W9-ADA-784

CARMELITE MONASTERY
LIBRARY
SARANAC LAKE, N.Y.

THE PASSION OF THE
INFANT CHRIST

NIHIL OBSTAT: Patricius Morris, S.T.D., L.S.T.

IMPRIMATUR: E. Morrough Bernard
                                    Vic. Gen.

Westmonasterii, Die 25 Januarii, 1949

The Passion *of the* Infant Christ

CARYLL HOUSELANDER

SHEED & WARD · *New York* · 1949

COPYRIGHT, 1949, BY SHEED & WARD, INC.

PRINTED IN THE UNITED STATES OF AMERICA
BY J. J. LITTLE & IVES COMPANY, NEW YORK

TO CLARE

INTRODUCTION

THERE are some truths which need to be told over and over again.

Our Lord repeated certain truths about Himself and used certain images of Himself over and over again, like the rhyme in a song. Repetition not only instills an idea into our minds, but it has the same power that rhythm has, to make the idea part of us and dear to us, even when it is hard in itself: and this gently and easily, just as a tune heard many times, sometimes quite unconsciously, becomes part of us and dear to us.

But there is a difference between Christ's repetition and ours. He speaks creative words because He is God, and because, as man, He is a poet whom no other poet has ever come near to: His words echo and re-echo through the human heart. We, on the other hand, tend to become tedious in repetition, even when the thing that we are saying concerns God and is beautiful in itself.

Yet, everyone who writes about the Christ-life knows that unless certain things are repeated in every book he writes, much in it, or all in it, will be almost meaningless to many who read it.

This is just such a book, and since the basic fact of the Christ-life, which is the key to everything in it, is the Indwelling Presence of Christ in us, I will repeat not something I have written about it before, but Our Lord's own words telling us of it, on the night before He died:

". . . It is the truth-giving Spirit, for whom the world can find no room, because it cannot see him, cannot recognize him . . . he will be continually at your side, nay, he will be in you." (John xiv. 17.)

". . . When that day comes, you will learn for yourselves that I am in my Father, and you are in me, and I am in you." (John xiv. 20.)

". . . You have only to live on in me, and I will live on in you." (John xv. 4.)

"I am the vine, you are its branches; if a man lives on in me, and I in him, then he will yield abundant fruit; separated from me, you have no power to do anything." (John xv. 5.)

"I have bestowed my love upon you, just as my Father has bestowed his love upon me; live on, then, in my love. You will live on in my love, if you keep my commandments, just as it is by keeping my Father's commandments that I live on in his love." (John xv. 8-10.)

CONTENTS

I	The Sown Field	1
II	Rest	17
III	Inscape of Thabor	29
IV	The Infant	44
V	The Passion of the Infant Christ	58
VI	Becoming Like Little Children	73
VII	Redemptive Childhood	89
VIII	Justice	101
IX	The Christ-Child's Mother	113
X	The Host Life	129

THE PASSION OF THE
INFANT CHRIST

CHAPTER ONE:
THE SOWN FIELD

Here is an image, he said, of the kingdom of heaven. There was a man who sowed his field with clean seed. . . . (Matthew xiii. 24.)

THE COUNTRYMAN is not impatient because the season of flowers and fruit is swiftly over and the winter is so long. He comes in early from his fields, to doze content while firelight weaves the long dusk with gold. He is as conscious of life in winter, when the crust of the earth is iron and not a leaf is on the hedges, as he is when the fields are green and the bough is white.

He has lived through cruel winters and heard old wives moaning full of foreboding for the spring; he has seen frost and flood and driving wind alternating through the dark months; but he knows that with spring the snowdrop comes again, and the pale drift of crocus and the delicate green blade of his early wheat.

He knows that the life sleeping in the earth is stronger than anything that can assail it, that the life that is in all living is stronger than death. That is the knowledge which is the root of his peace.

The mystery of the seed is his. It is one, but multiple;

dry, but contains the water of life; little, but fills the earth. Black, but is white bread. It is within the ripe ear of wheat, and the ripe ear of wheat is within it. Scattered on the wind, it is not lost, but carries life wherever the wind blows.

It sows the meadows and the woods. It sows the cleft in the rock. It sows the roadside and the ditch. It sows the dust-heaps in the cities.

Buried, it springs from the grave, a green herb of life. It is the symbol of Christ and the Kingdom of Heaven.

While the seed sleeps it grows. The season of the sleeping seed is the season of man's rest. Rest is the condition of natural growth, equally it is the condition of supernatural life.

If Christ is to come to flower and bear fruit in individual lives, there must be seasons of rest in which there is almost no activity but the giving wholly of self to nourish the supernatural life; just as the earth in which the seed is buried is given to nourish the bread. But, and this is even more important, there must be a permanent state of inward rest, founded in the peace of mind which comes from complete trust.

A state of mind inducing such rest becomes habitual if we fold our thoughts upon the knowledge that in us is the seed of Christ-life; if we fold our whole being round this fact, as the earth is round the seed, our minds will be at rest.

"Here is an image, he said, of the kingdom of heaven. There was a man who sowed his field with clean seed. . . ."

God is the Divine Sower—the world is His field. He sowed it in the beginning with all our necessities. Bread, fruit, water, wine, linen, silk and wool; resin, crystal, gold and oil, salt and fire and light.

Before sin had brought pain into the world, God had hidden remedies for pain in it. Men would discover the gifts of the Divine Healer and call them by names as melodious as the names of the nine choirs of angels, camomile, hellebore, heartsease, thyme, verbena, lavender, dwale. Most wonderful of all there was bread. God rejoiced in the world that He had made: "And God saw all the things that he had made, and they were very good. . . ." The Creator had stored the world for man, and to man himself He had given a mind and a will that would enable him to respond to His love, but God's joy at the dawn of His creation was in more than this.

In His field He had one little plot apart, lying under snow where no foot had ever trodden, silent with the silence of snow, that no voice had ever broken. In it He sowed Living Bread.

This little plot was Our Lady. In her was sown the seed of Christ.

The good seed which God had sown was the seed of His Son's life.

When the newly created water still trembled in the breath of the Spirit, and the seed was still hidden and all the wheat hidden in it, God saw His harvests. He saw the fields of ripe corn that would be irrigated by the Water of life, the bound stooks, the grain sifted and gathered into His barns. He saw the green wheat springing up everywhere, from the most unlikely places on earth; not only from remote villages and hamlets, where no one would trample on it, but from the thickly populated cities, forcing its way up between the paving stones. Trampled, but lifting itself up when the Sun, that was His own love, shone upon it. In the narrow streets of swarming slums, in the yards of tenements and prisons, from the ruins of men's homes destroyed by men. Whenever the world grew old, the green fields renewed it, whenever it grew drab, the burnished harvests were its splendour.

What is this wheat with which God has sown His field? Christ answered that question plainly, it is Himself. It is the Christ-life given to those who will take it; Christ is the bread that gives life to the world. Here are His own words: "It is I who am the bread of life." (John vi. 35.)

"God's gift of bread comes down from heaven and gives life to the whole world. . . . I myself am the living bread that has come down from heaven. If anyone eats of this bread, he shall live for ever. And now, what is this bread which I am to give? It is my flesh, given for the life of the world." (John vi. 33, 51-52.)

When Adam sinned, involving us all in sin and suffering, the punishment given to him and to his descendants was this: "In the sweat of your face, you shall eat bread." But even while those words still sounded in the ears of Eve, God looked on another woman, in whom the seed would be hidden, which would prove His punishment to be His mercy.

Already Love and death were face to face. In the design of God, the mother of Christ, before time, before light was created, was facing the darkness of death, pregnant with the life of the world, clothed in the sun, standing upon the moon, the head of the serpent already crushed under her foot:

"And now, in heaven, a great portent appeared; a woman that wore the sun for her mantle, with the moon under her

n by a driving storm that has uprooted trees, he has
a wild flower lift its ring of thin petals, tethered only
a stem like a thread of green silk; and more wonderful
an that and more certain, year after year he sees the first
elicate green spear of wheat pierce the hard crust of the
eavy earth and break its way through into the light.

How often he has held a grain of that wheat in his hand,
and in that grain the germ of life!

The life in the wheat means his own life to him, but so
much more than simply not being dead! It means the glad-
ness of his life: the delight that he has in his work, the brac-
ing of his body to the frost in the morning air, the stretch
and ripple of his muscles, his enjoyment of food and drink,
the blessedness of sleep. The answer of his senses to the
loveliness of the world around him, the sight of his roses in
the dew, the smell of his apples in the loft, the touch of his
children's hair, the volume of infinitesimal sound that fills
his silence; his awareness of the wonder of life on earth,
which comes to him from the response of the life in him to
the life around him.

It means, too, the colour of his face and his throat and his
arms, the long ropes of his muscles, the strength and line and
sinew in his large hard hands, the goodness and strength and
beauty of his own being, which attracts others to him, which
brings the love to him that is the core of his life, and give
him the fruitfulness of his love. Moreover this life of t
wheat within him gives him the strength of restraint,
power to pity and comfort, to face and accept his resp
bilities, to carry the burdens of his family.

feet, and a crown of twelve stars about
lypse xii. 1.)

"In the sweat of your face shall you eat bre
the mercy of the punishment, that through
would begin to know God, even before the ful.
His love was given to the world, or to them ind

When the revelation came it would be, in spite
within depth of mystery, one that came, at lea
countryman, as something familiar, in a sense already
like the reawakening of a sleeping memory of childh

The man who grows wheat, who ploughs and sov
reaps, who sets his pace to the rhythm and time of
of light, to seasons of gestation and birth, death and r
rection; who measures by the shadows of the sun and ca
lates by the width of the skies, lives, even if he does n
fully realize it, in harmony with the Eternal Law of Love

By a beautiful paradox he touches the intangible with his
hands and sees the invisible with his eyes. He sees the wonder
of life in the frailest living, how certain flowers and fruits,
and certain crops and birds and insects, are in the keeping
of some unseen power, before he learns that *everything* that
has life is in the keeping of infinite love, and that nothing,
even when it dies, is forsaken by that love. If he learnt for
the first time that, to this hidden Power, every bird is individual, that not one can fall to the earth by chance, and
that every stem of grass is valued for its own intrinsic loveliness, he would feel no surprise. He has learnt to observe
as carefully and accurately as a painter. He has seen evidence
of this personal love. Sometimes in his wet fields, beaten

More even than this, it is not only in him, this life that good bread gives, it is in his wife and children and friends. One life in them all. Not only does he share it with them and through it is in intimate communion with them, but in a true sense he has given it to them, by giving his body to the earth. He gave his body to be their bread, when he wrestled with storm and drought, with frost and scorching heat. When he worked until darkness covered his land, when the sweat ran down his face as he tilled the earth.

He can look at his children gathered round the tea table in his cottage, beautiful in the ring of the lamp's light, with their bleached hair like locks of flax, and their russet and golden skin, truly children of the fields of wheat, and he can know that, not only is he their father, who gave them life, but the labouring man who has given them the joy and the health and the beauty of their life, in giving his body to the sowing and growing and reaping of their bread.

This gives a wholly new meaning to the idea of earning a living. It is not, or should not be, just earning a "living wage," but working for a sacramental life, part of, but only part of, the answer to the petition that Christ put onto our lips "Give us this day our daily bread!"

"Here is an image, he said, of the kingdom of heaven. There was a man who sowed his field with clean seed. . . ." God has sown the world with living bread, He has sown the seed of Christ in the Virgin Mother. He is the Father who has given us life, and Christ, who is God made man, is the labourer in the Father's field. "A Sower went out to sow"— the countryman has his Divine prototype in Christ our Lord. Christ is the sower who went out to sow, who, having seen the green corn ripen to red, went out to reap, and having reaped and bound and threshed, sowed the earth again with the seed of His own blood, that the harvest might never fail. The labourer in the harvest, whose garment is stained purple, and whose seed is crimson. The ploughman who dug the furrows deep in His own body, and cleft the hard loam of human nature, cleaving His own heart.

He gave His Body to be our bread. From the moment when the Holy Spirit came upon Mary, and she conceived the Son of God, His body was given to us. Given in the first instance, just as the seed of bread is given by being buried in the earth, the seed of Christ, the Bread of Life, was hidden in the darkness, buried in the dust of human nature.

"In the sweat of your face you shall eat bread." The man who has known the splendour of his own integration through work, and the joy of dedicating his own body to those whom he loves in earning their bread, realizes the mercy in the punishment, but how incomparably greater the mercy is when Christ, the Redeemer, is the labourer in His Father's field. Christ took that punishment to Himself; He made human nature His own; He stood before God as all men, with all their sins upon Him, with the whole punishment to be suffered.

From the moment of His conception Christ was earning the bread of life for us; in His acceptance of suffering in infancy, in His own necessity, His hunger and thirst, His need for sleep. As a small child learning slowly and painstakingly to control and use His hands—He who had made the world; as a boy working at the bench, sweeping up the shavings in the workshop; as a young man resisting temptation, refusing to turn stones to bread, that the Living Bread might be sifted and threshed for us. In long journeys on foot and long days, meeting the incessant demands of the crowds; in the agony before His passion, when the sweat of His face ran down onto the ground in drops of blood, and in the consummation of His labours on the cross.

When, at the last supper, Christ took the bread into His hands and gave it to us, changed into His body, He gave us His flesh and blood, His Divinity and Humanity, for these are inseparable in Him, and He gave us Himself.

He gave us Himself, that is what the "Christ-life" means; it means that Christ Himself is the life of our souls. Our souls are alive because Christ is in them.

How much more this means than only not being dead! It means that just as the countryman's bread-given life gives colour and radiance and purpose to everything he does, Christ's life in us gives the colour and radiance and purpose of Christ to everything that we do.

Just as the countryman, with sharpened senses and perceptions, touches the intangible with his human hands and sees the invisible with his human eyes, we touch the intangible with Christ's hands, and see the invisible, the veiled face of the Creator in the creation, with Christ's eyes.

Much more than this, our human relationships with one another are a giving of Christ to one another, and a receiving of Christ from one another.

Christ gave us His life by means of His body. He is the Word of God, the word telling God's love. The means that He used was, and is, His body.

It was by the helplessness of His infant body that Christ first won human love, by His necessities that He bound His first lovers to Him.

The means He used were the most ordinary, the most natural: His voice, the words that He spoke, the expression on His face, the glance of His eyes. For two thousand years those who compromise have been haunted by the expression of Christ's face showing that he loved a certain young man: "Then Jesus fastened his eyes on him, and conceived a love for him" (Mark x. 21.); and the weak have been followed by the eyes that looked at Peter when the cock crowed: "And the Lord turned, and looked at Peter; and Peter remembered what the Lord had said to him, Before cock-crow, thou wilt thrice disown me. And Peter went out, and wept bitterly." (Luke xxii. 61, 62.)

He healed by the touch of His hands, by His journeys on foot. He redeemed not only by His pain and weariness and the sharp anguish of temptation experienced in mind and body, but by the delight that He felt in the loveliness of the earth and sky, the birds, the fields, the movement of water and waves.

He gave us the life of His body, in dying; and when He had risen from the dead, His ordinariness was almost more astonishing than His resurrection. He would not let His glory blind us to the way that His risen life was to be lived in us; we must not imagine that now He was only a spirit and that His life in us was to be only spiritual, the "living bread" only a memorial or a symbol: He made the doubter, Thomas, feel the wounds in His body; He warned the still emotional Magdalene that His *was* still a real body and not yet ascended to Heaven; He still used words, ordinary human words, to teach the things that men had not learnt, even from His resurrection; He still ate and drank.

In this life we cannot separate our souls from our bodies. They are so interrelated that for all practical purposes they are one. We live our Christ-life through our bodies. Just as His body was the means by which He offered Himself as a sacrifice to His Father, and gave Himself as our life to us, so by means of our bodies we can offer Christ to the Father and give Him to one another.

Our supernatural life is our natural life with Christ given to it, inseparable from Christ, as the Divinity and Humanity of Christ are inseparable in Him, and as our souls and bodies in this life are inseparable from one another in us.

Because Christ has given Himself to us our lives have the redemptive quality of His, and our relationships with one another are a communion in Him. They are a meeting and oneing of Christ with Christ, an impact of unimaginable love, the never ceasing generation and increase of Eternal Love on earth, the fulfilment of Christ's words: "I came that they should have life and have it more abundantly."

We live our Christ-life, offer our Christ to God, and give Christ to one another, by the means that Christ used on earth, by natural means; we give Him with our hands and eyes and ears, with the words we speak, the journeys we make, by our human friendships and human loves.

It is even truer to say that to our eyes Christ has given His eyes, to our ears He has given His ears, to our words He has given His words, to our hands He has given His hands, to our pain He has given His pain, to our hearts He has given His heart.

We see then through His eyes, listen with His ears, speak with His words, work with His hands, suffer with His suffering, rejoice with His joy, love with His heart.

It stands to reason that if we surrender our will to God's will, we will make our lives the echo of Our Lady's prayer, "Be it done to me according to your word"—that is to say, may Christ live in me the life He wants to live in me, where, with whom, and how He wants to live it.

Christ in us attracts to us those whom we can truly love, He radiates from those in whom He abides; but He is not only the beauty of life but its strength, it is He who gives the restraint and the tenderness that are the security of passion. It is His strength in us which makes us able to accept responsibilities and to bear one another's burdens.

Bodily temptations, which by their nature humiliate us, because they seem to soil us even as we resist them, are transformed by Christ in us, for it is Christ in us who resists, who refuses to turn stones into bread.

Not only those parts of life that are difficult and painful, but joy too is our Christ-life. If we see with His eyes, we see the loveliness of this earth, of skies and water and flowers and stars, with vision and sensitivity unimaginable otherwise. If we work with His hands, there is no work that is without dignity; whether it is a sheet of typing, scrubbing a floor, making a pie, doing a page of figures, carving a statue, playing the piano, or anything else, it is the work of Christ's hands. It would be incredible if people knowing that they work with His hands did any work that is shoddy and careless, or is not the best that they can do; whatever they do or make will be warm and living from their touch.

As to our love, it cannot fail to be creative love if it is Christ's. Loves that we had supposed to have no importance but for ourselves, love between husband and wife, parents and children, sisters and brothers, the love of friends, all these natural loves, if we love with Christ's heart, increase the life of the world, and build up the Kingdom of Heaven here on earth. That harder love to achieve, the love of our enemies, of those who hate us and persecute us, does not merely bring us pardon in our own sins, but it is redemptive, it has a reach as wide as the cross, and not only brings mercy to those who are its object, but to the whole world.

Everyone who lives the Christ-life, and therefore loves with the heart of Christ, is adding to the divine love in the world, which is the only force opposed to hate; whether they love their betrothed, their wife or children or their enemy; whether their love is happy and fulfilled or is one that they must forego and seem to frustrate, they are adding to the sum total of the love that is redeeming the world. "Here is an image, he said, of the kingdom of heaven. There was a man who sowed his field with clean seed. . . ."

Christ is that good seed with which our humanity is sown. Just as He chose to be subject to His own law of nature in His own life on earth, He chooses to be subject to the same law in His life in our souls. That is the condition of the growth of the Christ-life in us, from the seed to the flower, from the flower to the fruit: "Believe me when I tell you this; a grain of wheat must fall into the ground and die, or else it remains nothing more than a grain of wheat; but if it dies, then it yields rich fruit. . . ." (John xii. 24.)

The grain of wheat, which is our Christ-life, is subject to the same law. It must be buried in the earth. It must be in darkness. Its growing must be in rest.

It must be buried in earth, that is, in us, who are made from the earth. The seed of Christ is not buried in angels, but in men. It is to flower and bear fruit through human experience. Through our loves, our work, our sorrows, our joys, our temptations. It is to be literally our living and our dying. We are the soil of the divine seed, there is no other. The flowering of Christ in us does not depend upon pious exercises, on good works outside our daily life, on an amateur practice of religion in our leisure time. It is in the marrow of our bones, in the experience of our daily life.

The seed is in darkness: the darkness of sorrow, the darkness of faith.

There are those who think that only when material misery is done away with, and there is security for everyone, will Christ come into His own in men's lives. "Seek ye first all these other things and the Kingdom of Heaven shall be added to you" is the faith of this century.

Christ was born not because there was joy in the world, but because there was suffering in it. Not to riches, but to poverty. Not to satiety, but to hunger and thirst. Not to security, but to danger, to exile, to homelessness, to destitution and crucifixion.

His incarnation now, in us, is in the suffering world as it is; it is not reserved for a Utopia that will never be; it does not differ from His first coming in Bethlehem, His birth in squalor, in dire poverty, in a strange city. It is the same birth here and now. There is incarnation always, everywhere.

The law of growth is rest. We must be content in winter to wait patiently through the long bleak season in which we experience nothing whatever of the sweetness or realization of the Divine Presence, believing the truth, that these seasons which seem to be the most empty are the most pregnant with life. It is in them that the Christ-life is growing in us, laying hold of our soil with strong roots that thrust deeper and deeper, drawing down the blessed rain of mercy and the sun of Eternal Love through our darkness and heaviness and hardness, to irrigate and warm those roots.

The soil must not be disturbed. Above all we must not disturb it ourselves by our own egoism. We must not turn it over and dig it up by anxieties and scruples, we must not shift it by fretting for a sense of personal perfection; to feel sinless that we may feel free from the pain of guilt and anxiety; to feel pure for the sake of vanity; to be reassured of the hidden presence of Christ in us by experiencing sensible consolation.

The seed must *rest* in the earth. We must allow the Christ-life to grow in us in rest. Our whole being must fold upon Christ's rest in us, as the earth folds upon the seed.

The seed contains within itself all the beauty and strength and life of the wheat, all the springs and harvests that will be generated from it, but all this is the secret of the winter's sleep. Its green and gold is not seen, it can hardly be imagined now. Its rustling is not heard, it is as if it is forgotten, and will never be heard or remembered again. There is no faintest tremor of the movement of that tremendous life; yet, because the countryman knows that sleeping in the earth there is life, he himself is at rest.

During His winters in our soul, Christ is secret from us. Not only is He hidden from those around us, who in any case cannot see into our souls, but He is secret even from our own hearts. Now we cannot see or imagine His beauty; not the faintest echo of His word is heard in our minds, not the slightest vibration of His life stirs us. This is the moment of faith, the hour of growth, the supreme darkness, in which faith consents to God's law and allows Christ to grow in us, because He rests in us and we rest in Him. In faith Christ grows in us.

The sun penetrates the earth because the seed is buried in it, its rays strike down through the hard crust to draw up the flower into the day.

The ray of the Holy Spirit penetrates us because Christ is in us. The ray of the Holy Spirit is the fire and light that penetrates our lives and draws up the seed of Christ from out of our darkness, to flower in the Light of God. The love between Father and Son and Holy Spirit is our life and our peace and our rest. The life in all living is stronger than death.

"Let the Earth be opened and bud forth a Saviour."

CHAPTER TWO:
REST

Rest is not idleness; indeed, restlessness is the torment of idle people. It is not relaxation. Relaxation should never be necessary, because the nervous tension which makes it so should never be present.

Rest, far from being relaxation, is a culmination, a fullness of gathered peace, like the fullness and stillness of waters gathered to a flood tide.

Think of a child asleep in his mother's arms; the abandon with which he gives himself to sleep can only be because he has complete trust in the arms that hold him. He is not lying asleep on that heart because he is worn out with anxiety. He is asleep there because it is a delight to him to be asleep there. The mother rests too. She rests in his rest. Her mind and her body rest in him. His head fits into the crook of her curved arm. Their warmth is mingled like the warmth of two softly burning flames. She rocks to and fro, and her rocking is unconsciously timed by his breathing. Rest is a communion of love between them. It is a culmination of content. On the child's part utter trust in his mother, on the mother's part, sheer joy in the power of her love to sustain his life.

17

Such as this was the rest of God in the beginning of time, when He had created the world: "And on the seventh day God ended his work which he had made; and he rested on the seventh day from all his work which he had done." (Genesis ii. 2.)

God could not need rest. He could not be tired by creating the world. His rest was the Infinite Peace of Infinite Love. We have no words and no images to tell of the love between the three Persons of the Blessed Trinity; we say that the Third Person, the Holy Spirit, is the breath and being of Love itself, the sigh of utter contentment between the Father and the Son, but we know that neither our minds nor our hearts can begin to understand.

Neither have we any words to tell of God's love for us, but God has His Word; Christ is the Word telling how God loves the world. Everything that Christ said and did and experienced on earth is the Word saying "See how God loves you!"

Not content to be *a* human being, Christ wishes to be *each* human being, and is in fact born in the soul of every one who will receive Him; and in each one in whom He lives, whose life He lives, He is loved infinitely by the Father, loved as what He is, the only Son.

Looking at the world today, it is not easy to believe that everywhere Christ is born again, that God looks down on the wreckage and misery—the fiasco, if you like—that we have made of the world, and seeing us in the midst of it says "This is my well beloved Son!"

But this is so, and however difficult or however insignificant our life may seem to be, it is precious to God as Christ is precious to God. On each one in whom Christ lives, the whole of the infinite love of God is concentrated at every moment.

If this were realized, there could be no one who could not fulfil the first condition of rest, which is trust.

If it were not for Christ in us, we could not be able to trust, we are too weak; we could not believe in God's goodness if we had only ourselves to believe with, neither could we love one another if we had only ourselves to love with. We can trust God with Christ's trust in the Father, that is the trust which is our rest.

Our rest in a world that is full of unrest is Christ's trust in His Father; our peace in a world without peace is our surrender, complete as the surrender of the sleeping child to its mother, of the Christ in us, to God who is both Father and Mother.

This is not simply poetry, and there is no escape from reality in it. Christ came to take the burden of the suffering of the world on His own back, His love for His Father and for His Father's honour made Him take the world's debt on Himself; His love of men not only made Him live as a man among men, but made Him live the life of every man who allows Him to. Christ does not change. If He lives in us, He does so in order to motivate our lives and our actions by His own love of God and man.

There is a universality in Christ. He crowded such a wealth of experience into His short earthly life. Even in the matter of sin, though He never yielded, He knew fierce temptation; He took on Himself the sense of guilt and suffered the ultimate punishment for sin; He identified Himself with sinners. We are sharply limited, and most of us can only live one aspect of Christ's life at a time. There are some people who experience several aspects of Christ's life in their lifetime, and some who literally live it from His infancy, when His life first quickens their soul, and through all its stages of growth, until, through martyrdom or some unguessed equivalent, they die His death. In some He is momentarily transfigured, and afterwards it is certain that they will experience His desolation on the cross. In some He lives a life approximating to His exiled life in Egypt, in some His life as a worker, a preacher, a healer, in some He is homeless, in some He is in prison. In some He is stripped of His garments, in some He is nailed to the cross, in some—those who are in mortal sin—He is dead, and in some He is risen from the dead.

It is likely that there are those in whom a single unrecognized moment of Christ's life on earth prevails throughout their life; perhaps it is an unrecognized moment even to themselves, because it is one that has never been recorded in the gospels.

This book is mainly concerned with Christ's infancy and childhood, and His infancy and childhood in us; not because this is the only way in which He can be in us, for that it certainly is not, but because however else Christ is manifest in anyone's soul, His life in them must start by being simply the infant life, the small, miraculously helpless life trusted to them to foster, that it may grow.

In countless souls, particularly in England, where so many people live and die in almost complete ignorance of God and of themselves, Christ remains as an infant; He is in them but neglected, because they do not know the mystery of their own being.

It is not only in uninstructed people that the infant Christ is not fostered and does not grow to the full stature of their potential Christhood. There are very many Catholics who are so intent upon exterior activities, and on activities which are divorced from what should be their daily life, that they allow no rest either to themselves or those who are near them; they leave no part in the world's conversion to God, and forgetting His immemorial law, His *way* of acting in the world, they fail to surrender their lives to the infant Christ, at the time when their whole oneing with Christ depends upon just that surrender, which allows God to act in them in His own way. God not only asks them to rest in Him, but asks of them that He may rest in them. It is small wonder that the fruit of these zealous lives is so often the sour grapes of the prophecy.

Our age might well be known as the age of childhood. Children are the pivot both of man's malice and his love. On armies of exploited children ideologies have built their fever-ish hopes. Children have been persecuted, and it is only when it is to save children from starvation that men and women of all nations can still come together in great acts of love. It is to children and the truly childlike that Our Lady has come from Heaven in our own times, and to them that she has trusted her message of penance, as man's last hope.

Besides the ignorant and the restless, and every one at Baptism and at the beginning of their supernatural life, there are those who share in the circumstances of children, and who feel that because of it, there is nothing that they can do to mitigate the world's suffering. People whose lives seem to be circumscribed on every side, lives with little or no opportunities, people with no big gifts or big chances or even big ideas, as subject to obedience through, and to, circumstances, as little children, and as helpless.

There is in fact a huge force, a tremendous power for love, being neglected, not being used, at the time when it is needed as never before, and when every sign seems to be pointing to it and challenging it as the only answer—the power of the Infancy of Christ.

The Infant Christ is the whole Christ. Christ was not more God, more Christ, more man, on the cross than He was in His Mother's womb. His first tear, His first smile, His first breath, His first pulsation in the womb of His Mother, could have redeemed the world.

In fact, Christ chose the life of growth and work and suffering, and the death on the cross which we know; but by His own choice all this was to depend on a human being giving herself to Him in His infancy, giving her own humanity to the actual making of that infant's humanity and giving Him her life in which to rest.

If everyone in whom Christ lives at all, in whom He is an infant—which means anyone whose soul is alive at all—surrendered themselves to Him, resting in Him, that He might rest in them, in each one of them the world's redemption would begin as it began in Mary, the Mother of God.

Christ is formed in us, and we are formed into Christ, when we rest in Him and He rests in us.

In Advent Christ rested in Mary—still, silent, helpless,

utterly dependent. The Creator trusted Himself to His creature.

He trusted the expression of His love to her, the expression of God's love for the world, and of His love of His Father. Just as the work of His love would be trusted to us, in His life in us.

He was dumb, her voice was His voice. He was still, her footsteps were His journeys. He was blind, her eyes were His seeing. His hands were folded, her hands did the work of His hands. His life was her life, His heart-beat was the beating of her heart.

This was a foreshadowing of what the Incarnation would mean for us; for in us too, Christ rests as He rested in Mary. From the moment when the Christ-life is conceived in us, our life is intended for one thing, the expression of His love, His love for God and for the world. Our words are to be the words that He wants to speak, we must go to wherever He wants to go, we must see and look at whatever He wants to see and look at, the work that our hands do must be the work that His hands want to do, our life the living of His life, our loves the loving of His heart.

But there is the other aspect of this Advent of Christ's. While He remained hidden in Mary, His rest was a tremendous activity; He was making her into Himself, making Himself from her. From her eyes He was making the eyes that would weep over Jerusalem, that would shine upon the wild flowers, that would close in death and open in the morning of Resurrection. From her hands He was making the hands that would heal and raise the dead and be nailed to the cross. From her heart He was making the heart whose love would redeem the world.

The same thing happens when, allowing the Infant Christ to rest in us, we wait patiently on His own timing of His growth in us, and give Him just what He asks, the extremely simple things that are ourselves—our hands and feet, our eyes and ears, our words, our thoughts, our love. Not only does He grow in us, but we are formed into Him.

There are other points of Christ's rest, which He has stressed for us to see. One in particular underlines the part that trust in God plays in rest. This is His sleep in the boat that was tossing on a stormy sea. This was not the stiff, uneasy sleep that one would expect, it was the fearless, abandoned sleep of a child. Even (St. Mark tells us) He slept on a pillow. We are told, too, that He went onto the boat "just as He was." (Mark iv. 36.)

"Just as He was." No preparation for the storm which He knew was coming, no special protection from the cold and the drenching of the waves, no special warning to His apostles; why should they fear, or be forewarned, if the beloved Son of God rested among them?

"Master, art thou unconcerned?"
"Why are you faint-hearted? Have you still no faith?"
(Mark iv. 38, 40.)

Another episode of rest, full of significance for the modern apostle: Christ's rest by the well in Samaria. Here He gives Himself simply to natural fatigue. There are no heroics in this, the supreme hero; He sits down to rest. What follows has countless points for meditation. He asks the Samaritan woman for a drink of water—often someone in whom Christ is weary, in whom He is resting, asks us for something as simple as that. He said to her, "If thou knewest what God gives, and *who this is* that is saying to thee, give me to drink . . ." How often we too do not know *who it is,* who asks for a minimum of charity to a tired man! And at length, by revealing a little of His penetrating insight into her life, He sends the woman back to the village to interest them all, and the whole village invites Him to come to them. There is no other record of a whole village being converted, and this is not through His activities, but through His rest.

Christ prepared for the Incarnation by rest. He prepared for the Resurrection by rest. Rest in the womb of His Mother —rest in the tomb.

In the womb of His Mother His rest was secret, unfelt, unseen, making all who would live in Him into Himself. In the first place through Mary, His Mother, and her consent for us all, that He should be formed in her and by her humanity, as later he would be formed in every individual who endorsed her *Fiat:* "Be it done unto me, according to your word."

In the tomb, the profound, absolute rest of death, His rest was His growing towards the first Easter in the heart of the world, to His secret rising from the dead, and to His resurrections from the dead in countless souls to come, in whom He would be crucified and die.

At His death as at His birth, the circumstances of Christianity were the same as they are today. We hear it continually reiterated that this is a post-Christian world, that

Christianity is over, finished; that it is a failure—that Christ's teaching is impractical. That wherever the Church is powerful there is corruption. That priests are notoriously grasping. We are reminded that the persecutions in Catholic countries, which afflict the innocent, are provoked by the guilty.

In all this there is some truth. Where Christ is, Judas is. There always has been, and there always will be, a bloody hand to take the thirty pieces of silver. But it is curious that Christ is doubted because He is consistent, and does not change, but remains true in every detail to His Passion and its circumstances.

On the night of the first Good Friday Christianity looked like a failure—it was a post-Christian world; Jerusalem moaned in her sleep, uneasy, threatened by war that might destroy her. The Apostles had fled. Judas hung from a tree. Christ was dead. All that was left in the world to show that he had lived was the empty cross on which He had died.

The poor huddled together, frightened and miserable, in the slums of the city; the lepers cowered in their caves in despair; sinners trembled, flung back into the hands of men. What now of the dreams that the prophet-poet had imposed upon them? "Blessed are the poor"? What now of the pure of heart who should see God? They had seen the man who *said* that He was God nailed up like vermin, bruised, disfigured, flogged. His face covered in filth and blood and the spitting of the crowd. They had heard His voice, the same voice that had cried out so lyrically on the mountainside that not even a sparrow falls without the Father's knowledge, crying out: "My God, My God, why hast Thou forsaken me?"

Christ rested in the tomb. He had done all that He could do and given all that He had. He had trusted His Father and slept. Darkness in His eyes, silence in His ears, peace in His Heart.

Once He had slept in a boat that was tossed by storm. He slept now while a storm of evil tossed the world. The evil that flings itself in hatred against whatever is good, whatever is pure: the evil that seeks to kill God.

Christ slept. He had overcome the world, its storm could not touch the serenity of His consummated love. The hours moved slowly onwards through the terror and despair of that dark night, reaching out longingly to the moment of resurrection, the secret moment of ineffable love: the moment of the first heart-beat of the Risen Christ.

In that first beat of the heart of the man who had died, the resurrection of the whole world would be contained.

Neither Advent nor the tomb is Christ's final rest in the world.

He rests in the midst of the world now, in the Host.

He is as silent, as secret and hidden, in the Host as He was in Advent or in the tomb. He trusts himself to His creatures in the Host as He trusted himself to Our Lady in Advent, only then He gave Himself into the keeping of the one human creature who was sinless and in whom He could have His will, and now He gives Himself into the keeping of sinners.

In the Host He is immobile, dependent. He rests in the priest's hands, on the paten, in the tabernacle. He remains with us, resting in all the cities and all the lonely and unexpected places of the world. In little tin churches as well as the great cathedrals, in schools and hospitals and prisons and asylums, in concentration camps. Wherever human creatures are, He rests in their midst.

Just as His sleep in the boat that was threatened by the storm made His apostles ask Him: "Master art thou unconcerned?" there are those who are puzzled today by what looks like unconcern. It seems to them that once again Christ sleeps unconcerned in Peter's boat, which is threatened with the danger of sinking, but again the same answer comes to us across two thousand years: "Why are you faint-hearted? Have you still no faith?"

Christ could show His power and glory, He could show that the Host is God, He could break down the pride of those who have no fear of God. He does not; while injustice and arrogance prevail, He remains silent and helpless, and seems to do nothing at all.

It has always been Christ's way to come first in secret, to come in a hidden way, to be secret even in those in whom He abides, whose life He is, to be known first by His love, gradually becoming known by the quickening of His life within them and only afterwards by His face or by His power, by the word that commands the wind and the water.

The Host is resting among us in order that Christ may work the miracle of His love *in us,* changing us almost imperceptibly into Himself, that through *us* His love may overcome the world.

CHAPTER THREE:
INSCAPE OF THABOR

SNOW FALLS, and once again the wonder of childhood is upon us. At first a few separate flakes float down slowly, one by one; then more, faster and faster, filling our eyes with dazzling, dancing whiteness. The movement is more mysterious because it is silent: dancing, wild dancing, with no sound, like voiceless singing. If it made even the tiny tap of hail it would seem to fall into our world, but the silence is absolute; it is we who are walking in another world, a world in which we are ghosts. The falling flakes touch our faces with unimaginable lightness and melt on the faint warmth of our blood, at once elusive and intimate.

There is no one who does not sometimes return to his childhood, walking in the snow, back to the enchanted garden, where the Snow Man stands, at his slightly tipsy angle, with his mouth of red berries and his battered top-hat. There we meet Hansel and Gretel again, and the Snow Queen with her ice-blue eyes. We walk in the footsteps of King Wenceslaus to the poor man's cottage, and come suddenly upon St. Francis, the little poor man, making his snow bride. And Francis leads us to the crib and shows us the Divine Infant sleeping amidst stars and snow.

Every flake of snow is an inscape of the universe. Inscape is a word given to us by the poet Gerard Manley Hopkins. Students of his poetry discuss the exact meaning that he intended to give to it and to its even lovelier little sister, "instress." I use inscape to mean what it does for me, the pattern of the Universe within a little thing, like a flower, the ring on a bird's feather, a fish's scale, and so on. The pattern within it, not reflected on it, but integral to it, and whole and complete in it, so that in a sense it is true to say of such a little created thing, that its very being *is* the pattern of its Creator's mind.

The inscape in a snowflake is not in it once only, it is repeated in every minute particle of it; even our thought cannot follow it to its ultimate littleness. On the other hand, the pattern of the snowflake is a miniature of the design of the whole Universe, which repeats it, radiating round it, wider and wider, vaster and vaster, beyond our world, until the sun is its shining heart and the burning constellations its petals and tendrils; circle upon circle of visible and invisible beauty. Our vision fails, our thought fails, we cannot follow it home; we cannot reach its littleness or its vastness, for the end of both is God. It is the pattern in creation of the Creator, in whom is the being of all that is.

Snow is an enchantment laid upon our lives, woven into the lore of childhood, the magic of the human race. Yet the majority of us live and die without knowing what a snowflake looks like! Only a microscope can show it.

Men have laboured for long years in the forests of Siberia—forests that are like vast cathedrals of snow, with towering columns and pillars reaching up and up to crystal domes of stars—and have never guessed the loveliness of the snow-flake. Unless, perhaps, some of them, those martyrs who have died for their faith, have known it in the end.

Perhaps they, tied naked to the trees to be frozen to death, at the last suffered no more pain, but were granted the vision. Perhaps just at the end, when their love of God was almost consummated, they saw the snowflakes as they are.

Each one is a minute mandala, a circle of vibrant light radiating from a cross. Multitudinous though they are, there are no two alike—tiny ferns and stars and wild flowers of frost, each having its own exquisite design that is invisible to the naked eye. The essential beauty of each is not its texture or its pure whiteness or its silence or the delicacy of its touch, it is more than that. It is the perfection of the filigree design, the intricate yet simple loveliness of it, the mathematical precision and exactness of it, its balance and proportion and rhythm. It is a symbol of the beauty of the Law of Divine love. In it is hidden the inscape of the beauty of the Mind of God. It is the inscape of Thabor.

There was one dazzling moment, upon Mount Thabor, when those apostles who were to see Christ in His dereliction, suddenly and briefly saw the radiance of His Divinity, like a blaze of snow in the light of the sun: "He was transfigured in their presence, his face shining like the sun, and his garments becoming white as snow." (Matthew xvii. 2.)

The Apostles knew Christ as a man, one in whose presence they were remarkably at ease; in that moment they saw His glory, the very garments that He wore burning with His beauty, just as the world that He has made burns with the beauty that He is.

This is God's way with us, to hide and reveal Himself at the same time; to show His desire for man's love, making Himself accessible, even ordinary, that He may come close, yet at the same time playing a game of hide and seek, saying, "Seek and you shall find"; saying this with His human voice, and saying it with the things that He has created.

The old traditional fairy story is the story of God and the world: the King's Son who comes dressed as a beggar to win a poor girl for his bride, putting off His crown and His royal robes and coming empty handed, that she may receive Him without fear and may love Him for Himself alone.

God does not force His secrets upon us; He does not force His love upon us.

Obsessed as we are by propaganda, it is hard for us to rid ourselves of an unformulated idea of God Himself as a vast propagandist. The created universe is so beautiful, with so many different aspects of beauty, that we cannot at first realize that there is also the secret beauty, the beauty within the beauty, the inscape of love, secret and hidden in loveliness.

We imagine that God must show all that there is, flaunt it before our eyes like a banner to compel our conversion to Him. Otherwise, it seems to the vulgarity of our ignorance, there would be so much waste! But God does not approach us as a propagandist; He approaches us as a lover. Not only what we see with our eyes, but everything that He makes is beautiful, simply because God speaks only in His own language. In all that He causes to be is the beauty of His being.

The snowflake with its perfection of pattern and rhythm

is a showing of the Law of God, held still for a moment, caught by the touch of frost and held still for the time that it takes to melt away.

The Law is a Musical Law and, like the Kingdom of Heaven, it is within us.

All the laws that are made by man start from outside; but there is a law of God that starts from within us: it is the music of His creative love, its measure and beat and pause and stress, and it is within us because we are made in His image.

It is not a series of "don'ts"—not anything which stops our freedom and frustrates us. It is to our lives what form is to poetry; the rule and shape that changes a jumble of disconnected, meaningless words into a poem.

The law is the inscape of God in our own being, in our souls, in the movement of our blood-stream, in the beating of our hearts, in every cell in our body.

The rhythm of God is not like the man-made rhythm of machinery, a metallic beat that greed and fear is always trying to speed up. Sometimes boys and girls, riveted to the machines by our so-called "civilization," hear the beat of them incessantly—hammer, hammer, hammer, steel on steel beating in their brain. They hear it everywhere, in everything. In the noise of the train, in the hum of the traffic, in the blare of the dance bands. Sleep does not silence it. Sometimes, when their nerves are going to break, they become aware of the sound of their own heart beating and the hammer of the machine in it.

The rhythm of God's law is the gathering rhythm of song. It is set in great measures, not conflicting with human nature, but keeping time with it, and catching it up into its own torrent of beauty as a pebble is caught up in a running stream.

The deep primitive feelings of men and women have always found expression in rhythm.

Take the simplest expression of all: rocking. Moved unconsciously by some inner compulsion, young women rock their babies to sleep, and old women rock to and fro in their grief to put their hearts to sleep. They do not guess that they are moving together with the rocking of the sea, the swaying of the corn in the wind, the swinging of the boughs on the tree.

Ordinary speech gathers rhythm as feeling heightens, and all deep emotion breaks into song. Love and war, joy and sorrow, each has its song, from the lullaby that rocks the cradle to the keening for the dead.

Dancing, too, is a natural expression. Children and little animals dance spontaneously for joy; peasants and country people have a folk lore of dancing; savages have their ceremonial dances and their war dances. David danced in adoration, and a lovely legend tells how Mary, the Mother of God, when she was first taken to the Temple at four years old, danced for joy at the sight of the Holy of Holies.

The Law prevails in human nature, not only in our pulses and our blood-stream, but in the timing of every phase of life. There is both an inward and an outward timing of every phase of life. Childhood's years of enchantment are long years; maturity moves on at an even, steady pace; in old age, biologically, the pace is slowed down and, in the ordinary course of nature, we move slowly towards our longest sleep.

The supreme expression on earth of the rhythmic law of God is the Liturgy.

The poet is loved by his fellow men, because he gives them a voice; he gives words to the dumb love of the world and sings its song. The priest at the altar lifts the world's voice above the world to the feet of God.

There is no universal emotion that is not given a voice in the Liturgy; no individual experience that is not in it like the words in a poem. Love, joy, mourning, contrition: all have their expression, and so to the stronger passion of the soul, the longing for the descent of the Spirit and the adoration of God.

The whole cycle, from birth to death, from death to resurrection, moves through the Liturgy. It is an ever-returning procession through darkness into light; from the still birthnight of Christmas, ringing out suddenly with the shrill sweetness of the *Gloria,* to the flowering of the Cross and the dying seed-sowing of Good Friday:

> Crux fidelis, inter omnes
> Arbor una nobilis:
> Nulla, silva talem profert,
> Fronde, flore, germine.
>
> Dulce lignum, dulces clavos,
> Dulce pondus sustinet

thence to the descent into the grave, and the *De Profundis* of all generations who have died in Christ, Christ's sleep in the tomb, the awakening, the Resurrection, the thin flame burning in the dawn, the cry of *"Lumen Christi!"* shaking the heart of the world.

The Easter bells ring out to die away, not into silence but into the sound of waves lapping the sea-shore and the rushing of a mighty wind—the Risen life of Christ and the descent of the Spirit of Love.

The Liturgy expresses every passion, every emotion, every experience of the human heart. It is the song of the whole world; but it is also much more: it is the love-song of Christ in man, the voice of the Mystical Body of Christ lifted up to God. All our inarticulate longing and adoration, all our stammered, incoherent love, set in the tremendous metre of the Liturgy and lifted on the voice of Christ to our Heavenly Father.

All those things which manifest the beauty of the Law are integrated in the Liturgy: music, poetry, rhythm.

The slow, majestic movements of the celebrant at the altar, the great sign of the cross, the deep obeisance, the lifting up and wide spreading of the arms—all ordered, measured, disciplined, to be the medium of Christ's adoration.

The words, new on the priest's tongue at every Mass, are the words that have worn deep grooves in the human mind through the ages, like the river-beds worn in the rocks.

Prophecies of the budding forth of a Saviour, uttered thousands and thousands of years ago, are still, today, promises of the flowering of the wilderness of the human heart.

Because of the Incarnation, our natural life is supernaturalized.

Love has become incarnate: God has become human. Because of Christ's birth, a new stream of goodness is set flowing. Holiness has become the completion of nature: the fulfilling of the law.

Satan has not the power to incarnate himself in our nature, to make himself man, to be born of a woman. He must always work from outside; rabid because he is Hate, and Hate can never be incarnate as Love is incarnate in the world. Hate can never be born in generation after generation as Love is.

It may look as if evil is triumphant. But in reality there is always, from every outset of the devil, an element of frustration.

It is a tormenting thing, literally the torment of the damned, for Satan to be compelled to witness the indwelling of Divine Love, of Jesus Christ, in the dust that we are made of, and to see the substance of earthly things endowed, by the touch of His human hands and the warmth of His breath, with life-giving power, and these the most simple of substances, possessed by the Holy Poverty that makes them such fitting mediums of Grace: water and fire and chrism and oil and wine and bread and salt.

Satan has the intellect of an archangel. He has borne the dazzling name of Light. Surely he who was "Lucifer" must strain and agonize to make something equivalent to the Sacramental life for himself.

This may well be why he never ceases to tempt us to bodily sins. To sloth and gluttony, drunkenness and lust, and, with a shade more subtlety, to the pride of life; things which we pity and make excuses for as sins of weakness, not comparable in evil to those fierce passions of the mind that tear men's souls to tatters: pride, injustice, contempt.

Through the pitiful, snivelling sins of the flesh, the devil comes as close as he ever can to getting his sacramental system; he cannot *be* a human being with a body of his own; he cannot be born of a woman; he can never become a little child; but that which he cannot *be* he can possess.

We can give him flesh and blood to use; we can make our bodies his tools. We can give him, and often do, some material things to be his "sacramentals"; for example, much of our money, and most of our "great possessions." He cannot breathe life onto any substance, or bestow on it the grace to be a channel of life; but his touch can give a contagion of death to material things.

Nevertheless Satan is frustrated, though in his frustration human beings are destroyed. The very sins which he uses in his abortive attempt at some sort of travesty of the Incarnation not only do not give human nature to him, they weaken it in us who have it. They do not make the devil human, but they dehumanize men.

It is the commonest claim of those who try to justify indulgence in the sins of the flesh that, by doing so, they prove their humanity to themselves and to one another; that they enrich their nature by striking off every law that fetters their freedom.

Experience proves the opposite, over and over again with monotonous sameness.

It is just these people who, through a negative process, become dehumanized, divested of their humanity.

First they become depersonalized. This is because they depersonalize sexual life. It no longer means for them, *this* man, that woman, this chosen individual who is uniquely loved, in whom alone there is the consummation of life. The individual gives place simply to man, woman. Any man, any woman, no longer a particular person. Consequently there is no longer any objective love, but only self-love. Sex is robbed of its meaning, its spiritual potency and its glory.

Secondly, when the capacity to love is dead, they become dehumanized. They cut themselves off, *ipso facto,* not only from the Communion of Saints, but even from the Communion of Sinners.

The old sanctities and even the old necessities of human beings are held in contempt, the holiness and the permanence of marriage, that lasting love that is four walls and a roof, that is food and clothing, a pillow for the head, a light in the house, a rock under the feet.

Finally, they are denaturalized, they are no longer in the stream of life that pulses through the heart of the world; they have said with the Pharisee: "Thank God, I am not as other men," and, consequently, they have less of nature than the humble sinless animals. They have no part in earth or fire or water or stars, no part in the moon or the sun; they are not in harmony with the music of the universe, and that music is God's law. It is these people who boast that they accept no authority but the irresistible drive of their own primitive urges, who have, in fact, cut themselves off from the primitive splendour of human nature and all nature. Completely turned in on self, they forsake and betray their own children.

We English people have a frightening history of cruelty to children. We are a race of tradesmen who built our trade on the sweated labour of babes. We rose to industrial power on the breaking backs of little children, and it was their own fathers and mothers who drove them to the factories. Only the passing of a new law could prevent this; only threats of prison could protect literally thousands of children from their parents. Even so, long years went by before the public conscience stirred at all, and during those years countless little bodies were bent and twisted out of shape, crippled for life. To this day the penalty for a father's brutal ill-use of his own child is lighter than for robbing a rich man.

The law has stopped infant labour. Until a year ago, children of fourteen still worked in our factories; the age now is sixteen; but the law cannot prevent cruelty. Children are still broken by the brutality of their own parents; they are frequently ill-treated by foster-parents and in institutions founded to harbour them. All over the country nursery homes are filled with unwanted babies who are growing up without any knowledge of their mother's face or voice. There are hundreds of children whose parents took the opportunity of the evacuation of the cities in war-time, to disappear, abandoning them; to this day they remain unclaimed, forsaken.

But, exceeding all the rest, our most widespread cruelty to children is divorce. Go to the courts and study the lists of divorces; they increase day by day. Force your imagination back into the homes behind those brief statements of infidelity. In so many of those homes you will find a disillusioned, frightened child.

To small children, father and mother are certainty, home, love. They are all that God means to him; the firm ground under his feet, the reality of his life. They are, in fact, trustees of God's love for him: they must *be* God to him while he is still small.

It does not occur to the child that his father and mother *can* betray him, that one or both can abandon him, that someone else, a stranger, can take one of them away. It is in his nature to trust. For the child whose parents are faithful, it is an easy thing to love God and to grow up loving Him. But when the child is betrayed, by one or both his parents, what happens? Certainty, home, love are gone. There is no firm ground under his feet; there is no longer tangible reality to take hold of in his life. There is no God. When a mother destroys her child's trust in her, she endangers the faith in God of the man he will become. It is the legions of the children of the divorce courts who grow up to be delinquents, misfits, criminals, cynics, always on the defensive, always against authority: lonely enemies of mankind. They may find their way back to God, but it will be a very hard way, over stony ground. The mites from the factories had twisted backs; the children of the divorce courts have twisted souls.

It is better, says Christ our Lord, to have a stone tied round your neck and be thrown into the sea, than to scandalize the least of His little ones. What if it is the mother who scandalizes them?

Certainly Satan has cause for malicious exultation in the results of his attempt to achieve his sacramental system. But what irony for him in these very results; they not only fail to make Satan human, but they dehumanize those who are. He must remain outside of nature, outside of the harmony that motivates everything, from a man's heart to a star.

Only Love is incarnate. Goodness is natural because the Divine Child, who submitted Himself to the law of His Father's love, has made it so. Christ subjected Himself to the law of the seed in the earth, to the law of rest and growth. He was "one of the children of the year," growing through rest, secret in His Mother's womb, receiving the warmth of the sun through her, living the life of dependence, helplessness, littleness, darkness and silence, which, by a mystery of the Eternal Law, is the life of natural growth.

He submitted Himself to the law of nature; to the timing and rhythm of the musical law of God, with its pause and beat and stress.

His life in the womb was measured, like those of all the other children of the year, by a certain destined number of cycles of darkness and light, by the rising and the setting of the sun so many times, by the rise and ebb of so many tides, by a certain counted number of beats of His Mother's heart.

Who can think of the mystery of the snowflake, its loveliness, both secret and manifest, its gentleness, the moving lightness of its touch, the humility of its coming, and not think of the birth of the Infant Christ?

". . . a Son, whom he has appointed to inherit all things, just as it was through him that he created this world of time; a Son, who is the radiance of his Father's splendour, and the full expression of his being. . . ." (Hebrews i. 2, 3.)

CHAPTER FOUR:
THE INFANT

It is of absolute necessity for our peace that we surrender ourselves wholly to God. Most people want to do this, but they do not because they are afraid.

If, in their rasher moments of fervour, they have made heroic self-offerings, they go about their business afterwards distinctly uneasy, fearful that some catastrophe will overtake them in order to detach them from the earthly affections which they suppose to be hindering their perfection.

If, to seek reassurance, they turn to those saints who are said to have sanctified themselves through leading "ordinary" lives, they are even more perturbed by the extraordinary way in which they did so; the very thought, to give one example, of the hourly, even momentary, little sacrifices made by St. Theresa of Lisieux, opens up a terrifying prospect, all the more so because such lives are secret and without even the encouragement of friends. To think of oneself going on and on, denying self, giving up all the titbits, refusing oneself the relief of a little complaining or a little flattery, spending one's life in small coin down to the last farthing; this is beyond the power of human nature——at least of *our* human nature.

44

Both these anxieties can be put to rest by a little thought about God's approach to us, His way with human beings.

It is a way of detachment but of attachment; not a way of indifference but of love. He approaches not by catastrophes, but by gentleness; not demanding our surrender but winning it, if we put no obstacle, almost before we realize Who it is that sues for our love.

An obstacle would be a refusal of any love, a shutting of the door on those who want to come into our life. To put no obstacle is to have the door always open to everyone who has any need of us. "Behold!" Our Lord says, "I stand at the door and knock." An obstacle to surrendering to Him would simply be not to open the door. If we opened it and saw Who it is that knocks, we should not find it a difficult or a frightening thing to give Him what He asks of us.

The Old Testament, which many imagine to be the revelation of a terrifying God, is full of the gentleness of His approach. He comes as a "still, small voice"; He covers His face, lest it should wither away the light of a man's eyes by its majesty. He is compared to the coming of morning light and to rain falling upon the thirsty earth:

> We shall know and we shall follow on, that we may know the Lord. His going forth is prepared as the morning light, and he will come to us as the early and the latter rain to the earth. . . .
>
> (Osee vi. Good Friday Mass.)

Sometimes, indeed very often, His approach to us coincides with a catastrophe and is in the midst of it, and for that reason is hardly noticed. We are too intent on the din of the disaster to hear the "still, small voice," or we drown it with noisy tears. Disasters are not God's Will, they are the result of sin and opposed to God's Will; but in His mercy He does allow that the suffering resulting from them, though never the sin that caused them, can be caught up into His love and do good. Thus Christ's first coming on earth was in the midst of the disaster of the world's suffering caused by sin, and it was precisely to take hold of this suffering and transform it by love that He came.

How small and gentle His coming was. He came as an infant. The night in which He came was noisy and crowded; it is unlikely that, in the traffic of the travellers to Bethlehem, the tiny wail of the newly born could be heard.

God approaches gently, often secretly, always in love, never through violence and fear. He comes to us, as He Himself has told us, in those whom we know in our own lives. Very often we do not recognize Him. He comes in many people we do not like, in all who need what we can give, in all who have something to give us; and for our great comfort. He comes in those we love. In our fathers and mothers, our brothers and sisters, our friends and our children. Because this is so we may not be content ever to love with *only* natural love. We must also love everyone with a supernatural, sacramental love. We must love Christ in them with Christ's love in us. It would be well if those seeking perfection ceased trying so painstakingly to learn how *not* to love and learnt instead how to love well.

That other hindrance to surrender to God, the fearful prospect of abandoning ourselves to the pursuit of perfection even if we dared, can only be overcome by experiment; for those who live heroically through small things have *already surrendered* to God; their perseverance is not, as it seems to us, a continual strain; on the contrary, it is the repeated relief of giving spontaneous expression to love that is too great to be endured without it.

Knowing that God supplies all our necessities, and that one of our necessities is that we surrender to Him, we should not be surprised that He comes to us as an Infant: for surrender to an infant, any infant, is easy. Surely never did God receive more fully what is due to Him from man than when He was an infant. Every infant demands and receives the most complete self-giving that we are capable of. The perfection of surrender to God is Mary with the Infant Christ.

There is nothing more mysterious than infancy; nothing so small and yet so imperious. The Infancy of Christ has opened a way to us by which we can surrender self to Him absolutely, without putting too much pressure on our weak human nature.

Before a child is born the question which everyone asks is "What can I give him?" When he is born, he rejects every gift that is not the gift of self; everything that is not disinterested love. He rejects everything but that because that is the only thing he *can* receive.

Disinterested—not one-sided—love. One-sided love is never a consummated love, never a communion. It is a disintegrating, destructive thing; but disinterested love, objective love without conscious self-interest, is as near to perfection as anything human can be.

The first giving of this love to a newly born child is the

reshaping of our whole life, in its large essentials and in its every detail. Our environment, our habits, ourselves. The Infant demands everything and, trivial though everything may seem when set out and tabulated, the demand is all the more searching because it seizes upon our daily lives and every detail of which they are built up.

The sound of our voice must be modulated—the words that we use considered, our movements restrained, slowed down and trained to be both decisive and gentle.

Our rooms must be rearranged; everything that is superfluous and of no use to the Infant must be thrown out; only what is simple and necessary to him must remain, and what remains must be placed in the best position, not for us, but for him.

The temperature of the room, the warmth and the air must be adjusted to his fragile body, the light shaded for the eyes that have always been in darkness.

There must be a new timing of our lives, a more holy ordering of our time, which is no longer to be ruled by our impulses and caprice, but by the rhythm of the little child. We must learn to sleep lightly, aware of the moonlight and the stars, conscious even in our deepest sleep of a whimper from the infant and ready to respond to it. We must learn the saving habit of rising with, or a little before, dawn.

The rhythm of our own bodies must be brought into harmony with his. They must become part of the ordered procession of his day and night, his waking and feeding and sleeping. Our lives, because of his and like his, must include periods of silence and rest. We must return with him and through him to the lost rhythm of the stars and the seed.

All our senses must be given to him, and we must give him our hands. We must give him our hands, tending his needs and washing his clothes. In his service we must overcome all delicacy and fastidiousness.

For years I have been haunted by a single line in an unpublished poem which seems to me to be very close to a definition of sanctity:

"Hands that will dip in any water." *

I have seen the hands of a foster-mother chapped and bleeding from continually being dipped in hard water in frosty weather and have thought to myself that the stigmata are not, after all, reserved for a few rare mystics.

Our hands are one medium of the communion that must come about between us and the infant. They are fumbling and clumsy, yet they become acutely sensitive to every quiver of his body, to his dumb necessities. He teaches them by being himself. In continual contact with his defenceless sensitivity, our hands grow sensitive; they carry messages from the depths of his wordless consciousness, through our finger-tips, to our brain. Yet we remain aware of our clumsiness and the fallibility of our touch. Our hands only become really sensitive to his needs when we have so mingled our life in his that his pulses beat in ours, his blood flows in ours and his little bones are in the marrow of our bones.

Our clumsy hands remind us that we ourselves are in the hands of God. Our hands seek like a blind man's to learn an unknown world of consciousness through their finger-tips; in spite of our will of love our touch can hurt; but God's hands touch and hold with infallible love. He turns us this way and

* An unpublished poem by John Bartlett.

that, disposes us thus and thus, lifts us up and puts us down in infinite power and infinite pity and infinite knowledge. Every fibre of our being is known to Him, because His Being *is* our being.

In this re-ordering of our life, this re-setting of it to the pace of the infant's life and the new simplicity imposed on it, we ourselves are made new; we are restored to the lost wonder of childhood. We begin to respond again to morning and evening; to wake with the coming of light, to receive the stillness of the night in a draught of peace when darkness comes. We wake and sleep with birds and flowers and animals. We no longer contradict the sun, we no longer violate the stars. In and through a little child we become as little children, and while still on earth we enter into the Kingdom of Heaven.

In the service of the infant we are made whole. Every detail of our life is set by it into a single pattern and ordered by a single purpose. We are integrated by the singleness of one compelling love.

It is this wholeness which alone makes possible the complete surrender to God in which is the secret of our peace.

It demands of us voluntary poverty. The giving up of self, which is Holy Poverty. As long as we have something else to give, we always cling to self; but the infant lays his minute hand on that and rejects everything else.

This love, austere, childlike and poor, is life-giving love. I do not use the constantly abused and hackneyed word "creative" because nothing of ours is creative, not our love, nor our genius: God only can create, He only is Creator. But this love sustains life, that is its meaning and its purpose.

This is the point at which contemplation through our love of an infant begins.

Christ's immemorial plan is that His life shall survive until the end of time, as it began in Bethlehem, not in the great and powerful but in the lowliest and least:

> He hath put down the mighty from their seat and hath exalted the humble.

For two thousand years Christ has seized upon, inhabited and survived in the littlest and frailest.

The fostering of an infant's life is a thing of terror as well as of beauty. We are face to face with life at its most precious, housed in its frailest. That life depends for its survival upon us, upon the intelligence, the skill, the perseverance, the unceasing, untiring vigilance of our love.

It requires of us love that is as strong as the worn and hollowed rock, as delicate as the dew that trembles in it.

We stand on one side of the cradle, death stands on the other. The new life is still a spark, a spark that we kneel to fan with the warm breath of our own life, a spark that death could blow out so easily.

So is it, with the Christ-life in each of us and in the world. It is lodged in little ones, in the weakest and puniest, and love and death stand over it face to face. In the mysterious period of natural life between birth and babyhood, there is a parable of the Christ-life in the soul.

Infancy is something complete in itself. It is a mysterious growth from darkness to light. We are reminded again of the seed, of the thrust of the frail sapling life through the darkness and through the hard crust of the earth into the light.

In time, when the infant has become an established baby, the world will approach him from outside himself. Every new sound and sight and touch will be a new experience, not of himself alone, but of the world and himself. But while he is an infant, the human creature works his own way from inside his own darkness and aloneness outwards. He comes out of a world of darkness and silence and warmth into a world of painful light and noise and cold, of sensation and of pain. He is alone for a long time even in his mother's hands, the communion between them is not yet realized. He cannot yet respond, and no skill of hers can reach his deepest being in its primal darkness. He is here, in the room, in his little cot, yet he is away and aloof, just as the dying, whose cold hands we chafe with ours, are with us and yet are aeons and aeons away.

Both for the infant and the mother this time has an element of sorrow; for he is fighting his way through to the consciousness which is the beginning equally of joy and grief, of pleasure and pain, of life and death, and the way is a journey alone through darkness.

In the infant's first struggle to lay hold of his life, we can see in embryo the passion of man, the passion that recurs all through his life. Later it will be disguised, hidden by the grown man's reserve, but now it is naked, defenceless. The beginning of every life is a lonely fight with death, a dim shadow and showing of the Man who is in all men coming back from the tomb.

Our life in Christ is the risen life. We live in the life of

One who has overcome death, who has come back from the dead and laid hold of the world again with wounded hands; who has taken hold of its soil with wounded feet and loved it with the heart which it has already betrayed and broken and pierced.

Volumes of sentimentality are written about a baby's first smile. If we share the neurotic world's fear of sentiment, we shall miss its significance. It is the *"Consummatum est!"* of the naked showing of the Passion of Christ in man, which is at the heart of the mystery of infancy. The fight between life and death is consummated. The infant gives place to the baby, and he lays hold of the life of the risen Christ.

Gradually the uncertain hands that served the infant have brought him security; gradually the face that has so often leaned over him in the night has become known by him. On that face there has been a smile, a smile which no anxiety, no awareness of the fierce, suffering quality of life, could prevent, because it is the smile of joy that a man has been born into this world.

The child's first smile is a reflection, it is his and yet not his; it is the reflection of the mother's joy in his life, given back to her.

Birth and resurrection in their countless manifestations in the Body of Christ on earth bear a striking resemblance to His historical birth and resurrection.

The life of the baby following the life of the infant has a quality of reassuring ordinariness.

This quality of ordinariness in the Risen Life is an age-long reassurance: this Risen Jesus is no ghost, no apparition of terror and judgment bringing the frozen air of the grave with Him; this is a Man of flesh and blood, and this is God, endowing all that He touches with life, but touching what is ordinary, the substance of our life, making life supernatural, but living our natural daily life; eating and drinking with us, bidding us touch His wounds, not to reproach us with them, but to convince us that He is still the same Christ, who overcame death by dying: He is still the Word made flesh, who has lived all our lives, who has been wounded with all our wounds, and who has died all our deaths, and who has risen from the dead, a living man of flesh and blood still, to live in us and to live our ordinary lives.

Now the baby too has become ordinary; the Christ-life that was almost visible in him has become hidden, his own personality is already a disguise. The elemental miracle is not seen any more.

The mystery of the night is over; the procession through the darkness is accomplished; the peculiar beauty of infancy has gone for ever, and with it the minute face of sorrow, and the helplessness of the beautiful hands that were like sea anemones floating gently upwards in shallow water.

The spark of life that we fanned with our breath burns the single tiny flame that can enkindle the whole earth: the flame of Resurrection, *"Lumen Christi*—Light of Christ."

The service of the infant is a thing of love, therefore of joy. There is joy even in the saddest love, and the love of an infant, even when it has a quality of tragedy as in our days it too often has, is fundamentally joyful. It must be so, for it is the purest love of the purest life.

For a minute think back to the fear that the ordinary sinful human creature experiences in considering the saint's life of daily and momentary self-surrender to God. We have already reflected that for them such a life is not one of hardship and repression but of joy and relief.

So is it with ordinary people who foster the Christ-life in their souls, just as they would foster the life of an infant, housed in its human frailty, were such a thing asked of them.

No one, having received a little child, could count the cost. They could not list what must be done and given and given up for an infant. Every twenty-four hours could not be a period of trial made up from ceaseless small tortures.

But if anyone in such circumstances did count the cost in that way, turning the focus on self, their life would become insufferable; there would be that in it of which they must either rid themselves or else they will be broken by it.

But if the focus is on the infant, there is no hardship—the life of the mother, like the life of the saint, is not a life of repression but of the spontaneous, necessary expression of love.

If, in fostering the little seed of light which is Christ's life in us, the concentration is on self, on what we are giving and what we are suffering, then, indeed, we put ourselves into the place of the mother who is not a mother, the woman who counts the cost of loving her own child, and we force ourselves to face the choice of giving up the life in us, or of destroying ourselves in conflict between self and the life that has been given to us.

Christ came, and comes now, that we should have life and have it in its fullness, that we should be wholly human, wholly natural, wholly supernatural, that in all our loves He should be our life. If our mind and heart and eye are fixed not on self, but on the Christ-life in us, we shall realize the wonder of truth in His words: "My yoke is sweet and my burden is light."

Yet we know that of ourselves we can do nothing; how then can we hope to save this Life that is housed in our own weakness?

Many times every day we make the sign of the cross. Possibly we make it without considering what it means, beginning with the words "In the name of the Father . . .", but without reflecting on their meaning.

"In the name of the Father. . . ." In the name—that is, in the power—of the Father, we cherish the Christ-life in us.

More truly, it is the Father Himself who cherishes it. We must put the Infant Christ in our souls into the Father's arms. We must trust Him to hold us in His hands, to put us wherever we should be, to arrange the environment that is best for us, to rock us to sleep when we should sleep, to wake us when we should wake, to ease our pain when our pain should be eased, to feed us when we should be fed, to lift us up and to put us down according to the wisdom of everlasting love.

Everything felt for an infant by everyone in whom human nature is not dead is a dim reflection of God's love for the world. All that grace and miracle of sustaining love in us is His shadow in our soul. We are made in His image and likeness, but we have almost obliterated, almost effaced, His image in us by the grotesque travesties with which we have overlaid it. In the presence of infancy man is restored to the image of God.

Now, most wonderfully, we can learn God's care for us, by searching our own hearts.

The father and mother within us is only the faint image of the Father and Mother in God. He is the Father and Mother whose heart never sleeps, whose hands never lift from their works that they have made. Who has numbered the hairs on our heads. In whose humanity we are clothed as in a warm woollen garment. In whom we live as in our home. Who is our food and our drink, our shade in the heat, our comfort in sorrow, our healing when we are wounded, our light in darkness.

The Christ-life in us, the Infant Christ of our soul, is the only Begotten Son in the hands of God.

It is His creative love that has given us life, that sustains life, that is our life.

He it is who says: "Can a woman forget her infant, so as not to have pity on the son of her womb? And if she should forget, yet will I not forget thee." (Isaias xlix. 15.)

CHAPTER FIVE:

THE PASSION OF THE INFANT CHRIST

> *. . . and now the word of the prophets gives us more confidence than ever. It is with good reason that you are paying so much attention to that word; it will go on shining, like a lamp in some darkened room, until the dawn breaks, and the day-star rises in your hearts.* (II Peter i. 19.)

BETHLEHEM is the inscape of Calvary, just as the snowflake is the inscape of the universe.

As we have seen, the pattern of the universe in a snowflake is not only an accidental likeness, but is something essential to its being, entirely in every part of it, interpenetrating it.

This pattern is not all visible to the naked eye, but some aspects of it are; for example, in the dazzling movement of the snowflakes, as they spin round and round to earth, we see the perpetual rotation of the stars, and movement is as essentially in the pattern of the universe as symmetry.

But there is a design of extraordinary loveliness which cannot even be seen through an ordinary microscope, a repetition of the design of the whole snowflake in every minute particle of it, hiding the unity of the whole universe in less than a pinpoint of it. In the same way the Passion of the man Christ on Calvary is at once revealed and hidden in the Infant Christ in Bethlehem.

Some of this mystery is visible to our eyes, but much of it can only be known inwardly when, after we have knelt in wonder for a long time before that which we can see, Christ chooses to reveal it secretly to us, illuminating the darkness of the spirit with His light, as the Star of Bethlehem shone in the dark night of His birth.

The gospels are economical, direct, beautiful in their economy and austerity; they tell us the basic facts, that is all.

Mary and Joseph came from their home in Nazareth to Bethlehem to be enrolled. On the day of their arrival, the birth of Mary's child was due.

They could get no accommodation in Bethlehem, the inns were full. If they could have stayed at an ordinary inn, they would gladly have done so. They tried to get in but they were refused. For that reason they went to a stable, and there Jesus Christ was born, wrapped in "swaddling" bands and laid in a manger.

There is no mention of our Lord having been born in a stable, but only that there was no room for Him in the inn, and that He was laid in a manger.

There were shepherds outside Bethlehem, probably on the hills that looked down on to the little city, who were keeping night watches over their flocks.

An angel came to them. He came quite close and stood by them, and he told them that a Saviour was born. Then suddenly a host of angels—a multitude, the Gospel says—

appeared, not as we picture them in the sky but close to the shepherds, with the other who "stood by them." It is probable and pleasing that, since these angels stood close to the shepherds and their flocks, they were allowed to assume the human bodies which by nature they have not got.

When the angels had vanished, the shepherds went in haste to find the Infant, and they found Him lying in a manger.

After this wise men came from the East; they came following a star. Wise in astronomy, but over-simple in human affairs, for they fell at once to Herod's craft. He asked them where the child was to be born, and they would have come back to him, as he asked them to do, and have directed him to where the Infant Jesus lay; but they were told in a dream not to do so, and consequently they went back to their own country by another road, circumventing Herod.

These wise men adored the Infant and gave Him treasures: gold, frankincense and myrrh.

When they had gone, an angel came to Joseph in his sleep and warned him to fly from Herod into Egypt, and he took the Child and His Mother and fled into the darkness of the night.

Then Herod slew all the little boys of two and under who were in Bethlehem or its outskirts.

That is the story of the birth of Christ as the gospel tells it, but it has become part of the collective consciousness of mankind, invested with light and loveliness, which was certainly hidden in the darkness and crudity of Bethlehem, and supplied with details that are dear to the whole world, from another source. This other source however originates in the gospel too, and is an expression of truth. It is the Christmas crib, which is put up year after year in our churches and our homes.

The crib showing the nativity in all the cities and villages and Catholic homes of the world is not only there to commemorate Christ's first coming to earth, it is there as a symbol of Christ's birth *in* us.

Christmas does not only mean that God became man and was born as a human infant on a certain night in Bethlehem, two thousand years ago; it means that, but equally, that because of that, Christ is born in us today.

Christ is born in all the cities and villages, all the streets and homes of the world today. He is born in prosperous cities, lit up and noisy with pleasure, whereas in Bethlehem His crying is not heard. He is born among the ruins of devastated cities, where few would recognize Him without His crown of thorns.

He is born in New York, Berlin, Warsaw, Paris, London, everywhere where a single human soul repeats—even, perhaps, almost doubting it in themselves—Our Lady's *fiat*: "Be it done to me."

In an Anglican Church in a poor part of London, the painted background to the crib shows the actual street in which the church stands, with its narrow little houses, its crooked chimney pots, and its public house. It tells the people of that parish where Christ is born today.

Christ is not only born at Christmas, though it is at Christmas that we keep the Feast of the Incarnation; He is born day after day, in every infant or adult as they are baptized, in every sinner who is sorry for sin and is absolved, in everyone in whom God's grace quickens the supernatural life—which is the Christ-life—for the first or the millionth time.

The first crib was given to the faithful by St. Francis of Assisi in the year twelve hundred and twenty-three. It was his sermon for the Feast of the Nativity to the people of the little Italian town of Greccio.

The Saint had a real manger and hay brought and an ox and an ass led in. Mass was said over the manger, assisted by Francis as deacon, and all the townsfolk came with lights and the night was filled with their singing. The eye witness who tells this lovely incident says: "Men and beasts were filled with joy"; and again, "Verily in that hour Greccio became a new Bethlehem." We can say the same on any night, anywhere, in a tenement, prison, hospital, school, church; wherever Christ is born or reborn in a human life, that place becomes a new Bethlehem.

St. Francis could not separate Our Lord's Passion from His Nativity; he made the first crib, he said, "so that men should see with their own eyes the hardships He suffered as an infant."

A man who was present on that night had a vision; he saw the Infant Jesus lying dead in the manger, but when St. Francis came near, He awoke to life.

Thomas of Celano, who was one of the friars and who tells the story, makes a comment on this which could be taken with absolute sincerity as a comment on the world as it is today: "This vision was not meaningless, for had not the Child Jesus died the spiritual death of oblivion in many hearts, to be wakened to new life, and to reign for ever in the hearts by God's grace and the ministrations of St. Francis?"

The crib, besides showing the world something of the mystery of the Blessed Trinity, besides giving us the Mother of God and bringing the angels down to the earth, shows that the Incarnation embraces in its limitless tenderness even the humble animals.

Just as Adam's fall involved the whole animal world in suffering—"All things groan together with him . . ."—the birth of the new Adam brought its blessing to animals, paying fallen man's enormous debt of pity to beasts of burden, drawing them into the service and even close to the suffering of their creator and Lord.

On the night of His birth, when He first gave His body to us, lambs were brought to Christ. On the night before He died, when He gave us His body in the Holy Communion, He kept the ritual of the Paschal lamb.

The lowly beasts came into the stable to stand close to Mary and Joseph and warm them with their great shaggy flanks. The breath of cattle is fragrant with clover; old men and children believe that this is so because the ox was to breathe on the nakedness of the little Lord to warm Him.

At all events it was the yoke of the ox that Christ used as the symbol of the cross laid on the shoulders of all those who would follow Him through the ages. "Take my yoke upon yourselves, and learn from me; I am gentle and humble of heart; and you shall find rest for your souls. For my yoke is easy, and my burden is light." (Matthew xi. 28-30.)

A donkey stood by the manger, and Christ rode on a donkey on the eve of His passion; which, we are told, is the reason why every donkey has the cross marked out in soft dark fur on his grey back.

Long ago the prophet had foreseen the hour of Christ's birth and Christ's death in one inseparable vision:

> In the midst of two animals thou shalt be made known. When the years shall draw nigh thou shalt be known. When the time shall come, thou shalt be shown. (Habacuc iii. 2-3. *Good Friday, Mass of the Presanctified,* Tract.)

On Calvary He is set between two thieves. In Bethlehem He is set between two animals.

On Calvary He is poor, with the poverty of destitution. In Bethlehem He is poor, with the poverty of destitution. He is deprived of his home in Nazareth, the cradle made ready for Him is empty: "The foxes have holes and the birds of the air nests; but the Son of Man hath not where to lay his head." (Luke ix. 58; Matthew viii. 20.)

On Calvary He was naked, stripped of His garments and of all that He had. He was naked and stripped of all that He had in Bethlehem.

On Calvary He was stretched and straightened and fastened down to the Cross. In Bethlehem He was stretched out and straightened and fastened in swaddling bands.

On Calvary He was lifted up, helpless, and held up for men to look upon. In Bethlehem He was lifted up, helpless, to be gazed upon.

"Lo, if I be lifted up, I will draw all men to me!"

On Calvary He was laid upon a wooden cross. In Bethlehem He was laid within a wooden manger.

By the Cross stood Mary His Mother; by the crib knelt Mary His Mother.

He was crucified outside the city wall; He was born outside of His own village and crowded out of Bethlehem: "I am a worm and no man, the reproach of men, and the outcast of the people."

At His birth He was called "King of the Jews." At His death He was called "King of the Jews." The claim to be King threatened His life in Bethlehem. The claim to be King cost Him His life in Jerusalem. Three times the mysterious title is heavy with doom: at His birth, at His trial, at His death.

At His birth: ". . . there came wise men from the east to Jerusalem, saying, Where is he that is born king of the Jews? For we have seen his star in the east, and are come to adore him." (Matthew ii. 2.)

At His trial: "And Jesus stood before the governor, and the governor asked him, saying: Art thou the king of the Jews? Jesus saith to him: Thou sayest it." (Matthew xxvii. 11.)

At His death: "And they put over his head his cause written: THIS IS JESUS THE KING OF THE JEWS." (Matthew xxvii. 37.)

He was mocked at His birth by Herod. He was mocked at His death by the Roman soldiers; in both cases the derision was a mockery of adoration.

Herod was the pioneer of those hypocrites who, for their own pride, would slay the Christ-Child in the heart of the world: "Go and diligently inquire after the child, and when you have found him, bring me word again, that I also may come and adore him." (Matthew ii. 8.)

The Roman soldiers were the pioneers of those egoists who, for passing entertainment and sensation, ridicule and blaspheme the suffering Christ in the heart of man, motivated—like so much cruelty today—by group mentality: "Then the soldiers of the governor, taking Jesus into the hall, gathered together unto him the whole band. And stripping him, they put a scarlet cloak about him. And platting a crown of thorns, they put it upon his head, and a reed in his right hand. And bowing the knee before him, they mocked him, saying: Hail, King of the Jews. And spitting upon him, they took the reed and struck his head." (Matthew xxvii. 27-30.)

Two crowns are set side by side—a crown of gold at His birth, a crown of thorns at His death. The crown of gold is too hard and heavy for His infant head: His head bowed and died in the crown of thorns.

Tradition has named the wise men with three melodious names: Balthazar, Melchior and Caspar. To children they are three kings who travel under a solitary star, wearing their crowns and their royal robes, bringing scarlet and gold and ermine and blue clouds of incense into the stable.

One of the kings is a black man. His offering is myrrh, for he carries the sorrow of the coloured people in his humble, adoring heart.

At Bethlehem myrrh was brought to Him, and myrrh was brought to anoint His body for burial. Each time, it was brought by a rich man who came by night—first by the wise king and then by Nicodemus: "And Nicodemus also came (he who at the first came to Jesus by night), bringing a mixture of myrrh and aloes, about an hundred pound weight." (John xix. 39.)

Another king brought incense, frankincense that was poured into a censer of gold and lit with a flame, filling the stable with an aromatic smell to mingle with the smell of hay and the ox's breath of clover.

Myrrh and frankincense were poured out for Him in Bethlehem, and spikenard and ointment were poured over His body in Bethania, for His burial:

"And when Jesus was in Bethania, in the house of Simon the leper, there came to him a woman having an alabaster box of precious ointment and poured it on his head as he was at table. And the disciples seeing it had indignation, saying: To what purpose is this waste? For this might have been sold for much and given to the poor. And Jesus knowing it, said to them: Why do you trouble this woman? For she hath wrought a good work upon me. For the poor you have always with you; but me you have not always. For she in pouring this ointment upon my body hath done it for my burial." (Matthew xxvi. 6-12.)

There, in the stable at Bethlehem, began the lovely waste that is the extravagance of love; that is and will always be scandal to the loveless.

Already as the useless crown of gold that the infant's head could not support shone at His feet, clouds of incense hung in the rafters of the stable, and the air grew fragrant with the smell of myrrh, the box of precious ointment was broken to anoint the Beloved for His burial. Already before God the great cathedrals arose, growing up to Him like forests of stone. Jewels from the crowns of kings and queens were set in chalices of beaten gold. Already contemplatives, drawn by an inner compulsion mysterious as the migration of birds, flocked to God. Carmelites, Carthusians, Trappists, Poor Clares, were received into the Infant's open hands, and there nailed into the man's hands nailed to the cross. Nailed by the three vows that are the three nails that hold Christ in us, to the cross of suffering and love that redeems the world.

"To what purpose is this waste? For this might have been sold for much and given to the poor."

At Bethlehem He was wrapped in swaddling bands and laid in a manger; on Calvary He was wrapped in swaddling bands and laid in a tomb. Both the manger and the tomb were borrowed.

Both had been made for their owners. They were not made for Christ. All that had been prepared for Him God had set aside. God chose what men should give to His Son, and He chose things so shaped or worn to the givers' life that they had become part of them, so warm with the givers' touch that they could not be given without the giving of self.

Christ accepted those offerings in which self was given; not what man had made for Him, but what man had made for himself. The gifts with self at the core, involving the surrender of the giver's will, even in the choice of the gift.

So it is today and always. We would like to give God gifts of our own choosing which, even if they are in one sense part of our life, are yet things added on, on purpose to give, without having to pull up anything of ourself at the roots.

We are often surprised when, after we have offered God several litanies a day, and a pest of little mortifications, He chooses instead something that is really ourselves; our solitude for example, or the sweetness of the feeling of love; or, as is very frequent now, our home.

It is what *God* chooses that kindles in the crucible and burns the flame of love.

He accepted both straw and gold—He did not despise the humble animals, or the humility of their giving; He accepted the warm breath of the cattle on His cold hands and feet, the soft touch of the sheep's wool, the joy that shone from the violet eyes of the little red calves.

There was no distinction of colour or race or class or education or money in Bethlehem; kings and shepherds, coloured men and white men, angels and beasts adored together.

The treasure of kings lay at the foot of the manger with the sheepskin coats the shepherds had taken off to give and their scarlet gourds of milk and wine.

In Bethlehem the Mother of Christ gave Christ's human body to us. She had given her own flesh and blood to Him, to be His flesh and blood. Now she gave herself to us in Him; giving Him to us. She gave His body to cold, to thirst, to light and darkness, to sleep.

In Bethlehem began the thirst of Calvary, the terrible thirst of bloodlessness that withers the tongue and the hands and feet and the whole body. In Bethlehem came the infant blindness; and blindness came again on Calvary, filling Christ's eyes with the darkness of dying.

In Bethlehem Christ slept His first sleep in His Mother's arms; on Calvary, Christ slept His last sleep in His Mother's arms.

In the inscape of Calvary, in the Passion of the Infant Jesus we behold His resurrection from the dead.

Christ came out of the darkness of the womb. He was the Light of the World. He came to give the world life. The life of the whole world burnt in the tiny flame of an infant's life; it began the age-long fight with death in the least and frailest that human nature can be; in the helplessness, the littleness, the blindness of an infant, life prevailed. The Light of the World shone in darkness.

At Bethlehem Love and Death met in the body of Christ, and Love prevailed.

Over and over again in every human life, love and death meet face to face. No human power or splendour or strength, no material might or wealth, can overcome death—the death of the soul. But if the life in the soul is the tiniest spark of the life of Christ, love prevails and death is overcome in us.

Christ came out of the darkness of the tomb. He came back from the helplessness and blindness and silence of death, and His feet that walked on earth bore the wounds of death, and His hands that touched the flowers and the grass bore the wounds of death. He had overcome the world; He had died all our deaths and had overcome death. All over the world, in generation after generation, men rose from the dead; all over the world, everywhere, there was resurrection and Easter morning in the heart of man.

At Bethlehem angels stood among the flocks and round the stable door; angels stood beside the empty tomb.

The Message of the Incarnation is peace.

On the hills above Bethlehem the angels' song was Peace:

> "Glory be to God in the highest,
> And on earth,
> Peace to men of good will."

And Peace was the word on the tongue of the Risen Christ, His greeting to the world: "Peace be to you."

At the Nativity, it was to shepherds that the angels brought the message of peace, and shepherds who came first to the Divine Child.

On the night before He suffered Christ, keeping the Feast of the Paschal Lamb, gave His peace, the peace of the Lamb of God: "Peace I leave with you: my peace I give unto you." (John xiv. 27.)

When the season of the Risen Christ had come, warm with light and flower and fruit and the abundance of His Life, it was to a shepherd that Christ came, entrusting the giving of His love and life and peace to him.

He came to Peter, the shepherd of His own Flock, the Shepherd for all time of His shearlings and His sheep:

"Simon, Son of John, lovest thou me more than these?"

"Yea, Lord, thou knowest that I love thee."

"Feed my lambs."

"Simon, Son of John, lovest thou me?"

"Yea, Lord, thou knowest that I love thee!"

"Feed my lambs."

"Simon, Son of John, lovest thou me?"

"Lord, thou knowest all things; thou knowest that I love thee!"

"Feed my sheep."

CHAPTER SIX:

BECOMING LIKE LITTLE CHILDREN

> *Believe me, unless you become like little children again, you shall not enter the kingdom of heaven.* (Matthew xviii. 3.)

It is encouraging and pleasing that Our Lord does not tell us to remain, but to become, as little children. And that it is *little* children we are told to become like, not adolescents.

An ordinary child, who has not been warped by ill treating or spoiling, is, until he is ten years old, a more complete human being than he will ever be again. He possesses humility and simplicity, in the true sense of those much-abused words. He has the capacity for total joy and total surrender. No memory and no experience of the power of time to dull and to heal can take away one jot from his eternal now. His reactions to other people are absolute, his love is without alloy. His trust is without question or doubt. His values are true; he is untouched by the materialism of grown-up people. Even when he selects among the things that adults give to him as the things of a child, he shows the superior wisdom, and exquisite rightness, of a young child's values in his choice. He discards the expensive toys that are offered to him

73

in favour of those things which are useful or beautiful—or both—and which in some way mean communion with adults. For the little child loves adults, wholly beyond their deserts. Just before he leaves his childhood, he has, like a grace, an absorbed love for little things, like tiny shells, for their own loveliness.

Humility, which cannot be separated from real simplicity, is part of young childhood. Children do not become bitter because they are treated as little and insignificant: they take it for granted that they are so, and to them it is as necessary to love and to be loved as it is to eat and drink.

If we could go back to nurseries that are no more, and see what is left in them when the children went away, we should find traces of human nature in its essence, as convincing as those found in the caves, where the earliest known men left their signature of humanity in sanguine on the walls.

For the child under ten is, like the cave man, an artist and a poet, and, made as he is in the image and likeness of God, he has the elements of lover and father and mother within him.

In the nursery we would almost certainly find, among the discarded and broken toys from the big store, marvellous pictures drawn in coloured chalks, in which the sun has a smiling face and a halo of scarlet rays; a boat cut out of a small piece of soft wood; bricks built into a little house; marbles and shells; and, among the mutilated bodies of murdered rich dolls, one cherished old rag doll or moulted teddy bear that has been submitted to the glorious, fair wear and tear of love, which has flattened its nose but left it triumphant.

To go back to childhood means that we must get back true values, instead of those that are based on materialism, public opinion and snobbery; that we must regain simplicity and humility, that we must become makers and poets again, that we must regain the capacity to experience fully whatever we experience at all; and, above all, we must regain the courage that is partly a boundless zest for living and partly an unquestioning trust in an all-powerful love.

There are adults who do achieve this going back to childhood, but they are in the minority, because few have this trust and the courage it brings with it. Courage not only to take the necessary steps to return to childhood after we have grown up, but courage to grow up in the first place.

Those who fail to grow up do not remain children. What happens to them is this: they become fixed in their adolescence. They remain emotionally and mentally incomplete all their lives—perpetual adolescents.

Most of the few women who have achieved psychological maturity have at least one old school friend who is fixated in the upper fourth or the lower fifth; whose thought and interest and conversation is all concerned with the old days at school; whose emotions are those of a school girl. She suffers more than her mature friend is likely to realize. She is continually grieved because the other has outgrown her and is no longer even capable of thrilling to the old excitements and sentimentalities of her adolescence. She is constantly "hurt" by, and jealous of, the mature affections and wider interests whose claims her former "greatest friend" puts before her own. She looks back wistfully to the days when notes were exchanged under the desk, declaring total surrender to the tyranny of almost paranoic friendship, including pledges not even to be on speaking terms with potential rivals. This is one of the most obvious forms of perpetual adolescence; but pitiful though it is, it is far from being the most fatal.

This state is by no means confined to women; on the contrary, there are even more adolescent men, men who are dogged all through their lives by the schoolboy that they used to be. Sometimes it is a hearty, insensitive schoolboy, who thinks an excess of food or drink, or any other appetite, is amusing; but far more often it is an unhappy, shivering boy, who infects the man with the same fear of life that he brought to his first term at his public school.

The perpetual adolescent does not grow up because he—or she—is afraid to do so. Afraid of life: of grown-up responsibilities, of working for a living, of independence, of making decisions, of taking risks; afraid of falling in love, of making a home, of having children; afraid of sickness, of growing old and of dying.

Our Lord's words are a challenge. To become a child is a challenge to our courage. It demands, first of all, that we dare to grow up, to give ourselves to life, to accept life as it is—and above all, to accept ourselves as we are.

Many people are permanently humiliated because they cannot accept themselves as they think themselves to be. They are humiliated by a feeling of futility and frustration, which does not seem to fit in with their worldly success. It is not a fanciful feeling. They are people in whom the supernatural life is undeveloped and even unguessed. They feel—and rightly—that there are unrecognized depths within them, possibilities which no one knows of, and which they themselves cannot bring into the light. They know instinctively, though they would seldom admit it, that to be a man without spirituality is hardly to be a man at all, but the materialism of their environment has strangled their capacity for spirituality.

Hardly any man, however proudly carnal he may be, wishes to believe of himself that he has no religion at all. The man who does come near to that asserts and reasserts, with the overemphasis of the unconvinced, that he has his own religion.

Humiliated by their own not understood, but deeply felt, spiritual impotency, men try to compensate by material success. They try to fill the emptiness within themselves by money, position, flattery. They try to answer and quieten the unappeasable longing to achieve the glory of complete humanity by the achievement of human power; and a humiliated man who does manage to grasp power over other human beings is a potential danger to the world, far more terrible than an atom bomb or bacteriological warfare. For no man who does not nail his hands with the hands that nailed Christ to the Cross, and does not plunge himself into the magnitude of the littleness of the Infant Christ, is safe to exercise power.

Ideologies could not come into being without this epidemic humiliation, for they depend on a multitude of young men and young women identifying themselves with a human leader. Every member of the group accepts the ideas of the leader. He accepts the leader's mind and his conscience. He lives, not by his own conscience, his own will, but the conscience and will of the leader, until the time comes when he *has* no will but the leader's. He loses sight of his own lack of mind and of purpose, and of his own limitations and littleness, and he abandons all personal responsibility for his own thoughts and actions. He is always in fancy dress. He is always acting a part, and in time he really believes that he shares the force and genius of the leader. Thus, for a time, he has a drug to anaesthetize the ache of his own humiliation.

Even when a group is passive, group mentality fosters delusion and pride; but when the group is driven—or "led" —into action, it simply becomes the most dangerous and most horrible of all things, crowd mentality. Identified with a crowd, possessed by it, a man who is really just and temperate behaves like an irrational creature. He will blaspheme, lynch, murder, all without any sense of his personal responsibility. He is in worse case than a man who is drunk, for he is not only himself out of control, but has in him the uncontrolled evil in several hundreds or thousands of other men too.

Undoubtedly many who thronged the Way of the Cross hurled curses and insults at Christ only because they were possessed by a crowd. Had they had the strength to be alone, perhaps, like St. Veronica, they would have wiped the spitting of that crowd from the suffering face of Innocence. The only identification which deepens a man's awareness of his personal responsibility as a human being is identification with Christ. The only solidarity with others which enables an individual to be wholly himself, and yet really one with all other men, is the Mystical Body of Christ. This is less an organized than an organic oneness:

"A man's body is all one, though it has a number of different organs; and all this multitude of organs goes to make up one body; so it is with Christ. We too, all of us, have been baptized into a single body by the power of a single Spirit, Jews and Greeks, slaves and free men alike; we have all been given drink at a single source, the one Spirit. The body, after all, consists not of one organ but of many; if the foot should say, I am not the hand, and therefore I do not belong to the body, does it belong to the body any the less for that? If the ear should say, I am not the eye, and therefore I do not belong to the body, does it belong to the body any the less for that? Where would the power of hearing be, if the body were all eye? Or the power of smell, if the body were all ear? As it is, God has given each one of them its own position in the body, as he would. If the whole were one single organ, what would become of the body? Instead of that, we have a multitude of organs, and one body. The eye cannot say to the hand, I have no need of thee, or the head to the feet, I have no need of you. On the contrary, it is those parts of our body which seem most contemptible that are necessary to it. . . ." (I Corinthians xii. 12-23.)

It is not only the spiritually starved who are humiliated, and who escape from the realization of their grown-up responsibilities into perpetual adolescence, but also many pious people, Catholic and non-Catholic alike. There are countless people among them who will not accept themselves as they are, and who warp their own natures by dwelling continually on the supposed injustice which has made their destinies mediocre. They feel that but for cruel and frustrating circumstances they would have been famous. Had they been wealthy, or given a better education, they would have developed their talents and won recognition. Varying the theme, had not their pampered upbringing stifled initiative, had they been pricked on by the spur of poverty, like so many great men, they would have fulfilled their genius. They live with the grievance, refusing to use the talents that they have, because no one recognizes the talent they have not.

Others escape from their humiliation into daydreams of personal aggrandizement, a pathetic tendency often seen, as if under a microscope, in school children who, when the dramatization of illness and the telling and retelling of stories that they at last believe fails, will often resort simply to mystery, and mystery never fails. "I have a secret." And the secret is that they have no secret!

Grown-up people, too, resort to mysteries and wishful fantasies, and sometimes they not only dream and talk about them, but live them and thereby complicate other people's lives. There are people whose vanity is such that in times of danger they do not see the people around them objectively, but only themselves in the role of heroine, at the centre of things; and, only to support this role, take unnecessary and unwarrantable risks and compel others to take them with them.

Think, too, of the innumerable people who, in order to seem—to themselves as well as to others—to be richer than they are, or socially superior, or more successful, live lives of petty dishonesty; owing bills, often to those who are too poor to be kept waiting for their money, or money to friends who are too delicate to ask for it; living on credit; being underhanded and grasping in business; paying the minimum wages; living extravagantly themselves, while they let their obligations slide; shutting their eyes to the real needs of their unimportant neighbours and entertaining those from whom something may be gained; exploiting weakness and kindness wherever they find it; and desecrating themselves by deliberately childless marriages.

To keep up pretences, human beings will sacrifice their deepest human needs. What can have so complicated them, and made them so ill use themselves? They are complicated because the world is complicated, and they are trying to adjust themselves to the standards of the world.

All this is the exact opposite to the simplicity of childhood. Simplicity is not—as so many think, and, alas teach—silliness. Simplicity means not being complicated, not being double in any way, not deluding oneself or anyone else. The first exercise in simplicity is to accept oneself as one is. There are two tremendous results of this: one is humility; the other, that it enables other people to accept us as we are, and in this there is real charity.

People whose demand on others is simple and uncomplicated add to the life of the world. One of the main reasons for devitalization, depression and psychological tiredness is that we make complicated demands on one another.

Everyone has, so to speak, his individual income of psychological energy—some more, some less. Everyone, in his relations with other people, makes a demand on that energy. There are normal demands, which result in a fair give-and-take, and there are abnormal demands, which result in a dreadful deprivation. Some people cost us a lot of energy; they are expensive to know; unless we have abnormally high psychological energy, they exhaust us. Others make only the slightest demands, and others actually give.

The expensive people are those who, because they are not simple, make complicated demands; people to whom we cannot respond spontaneously and simply, without anxiety. They need not be abnormal to exact these complicated responses; it is enough that they should be untruthful, or touchy, or hypersensitive; or that they have an exaggerated idea of their own importance, or that they have a pose—one which may have become second nature, but is not what they really are. With all such people we are bound to experience a little hitch in our response. If we are not sure that what they say is true, we are embarrassed. In time, our relationship with them becomes unreal. If we have to consider every word or act in their company, in case it hurts their feelings or offends their dignity, or to act up to them in order to support their pose, we become strained by their society. They are costing us dearly in psychological energy.

The individual who is simple, who accepts himself as he is, makes only a minimum demand on others in their relations with him. His simplicity not only endows his own personality with unique beauty; it is also an act of real love. This is an example of the truth that whatever sanctifies our own soul does, at the same time, benefit everyone who comes into our life.

One immediate result of accepting ourselves as we are—which is becoming simple—is that we stop striving to reach a goal which means becoming something that the world admires, but which is not really worth while. Instead we realize the things that really do contribute to our happiness, and work for those. For example, we cease to want to be rich or successful or popular, and want instead the things that satisfy our deeper instincts; to be at home, to make things with our hands, to have time to see and wonder at the beauty of the earth, to love and to be loved.

To work for real human happiness implies unworldliness, the kind of unworldliness that is usually a characteristic of artists, who—in spite of glaring faults—prefer to be poor, that they may be able to make things of real beauty as they conceive it, rather than to suit themselves to the tastes and standards of the world.

To accept oneself as one is; to accept life as it is: these are the two basic elements of childhood's simplicity and humility. But it is one thing to say this and another to do it. What is involved? First of all, the abandoning of all unreality in ourselves. But even granted that we have the courage to face ourselves and to root out every trace of pretence, how shall we then tolerate the emptiness, the insignificance, that we built up our elaborate pretence to cover?

The answer is simple. If we are afraid to know ourselves for what we are, it is because we have not the least idea of what that is. It is because we have not the least idea of the miracle of life-giving love that we are. There is no pretence that can approach the wonder of the truth about us, no unreality that comes anywhere near the reality.

We are "other Christs." Our destiny is to live the Christ-life: to bring Christ's life into the world; to increase Christ's love in the world; to give Christ's peace to the world.

What contemptible pigmies our most exalted ambitions and fantasies are beside this, the reality!

The acceptance of life as it is must teach us trust and humility. Because every real experience of life is an experience of God. Every experience of God makes us realize our littleness, our need, our nothingness, but at the same time the miracle of Christ in us. Not only are we one of God's creatures—which is in itself a guarantee of His eternal creating love—but we are also His Christ, His only Son, the sole object of His whole love. These two facts balance the scales of trust. Our nothingness and our allness.

If, in the light of this knowledge, we give ourselves unreservedly to life, every phase of it, every experience in it, will lead us back to the inward heaven of spiritual childhood.

"All the way to Heaven is Heaven," says St. Catherine of Siena, and this is a thousand times true of the heaven of spiritual childhood, because it means becoming, not any child, but the Child Christ who is the life and the heaven of the soul.

Life should make full circle from birth to death that is rebirth. The ordinary experiences of adult life, offered to everyone if he will take them, are work, friendship, love, home, children, rest, old age and death. Within these—varying and alternating—poverty and riches, success and failure, forgiving and being forgiven, dependence on one another, illness and recovery, the illness and recovery of those whom we love, sometimes their deaths.

The experience at the core of every other, giving all the

other experiences their significance, making them fruitful, is simply love. When we love, even the sufferings that our love makes more acute throw us upon the heart of God and teach us the wisdom of childhood.

Poverty when those whom we love are dependent on us, illness when those whom we love are in danger of death, teach us our own insufficiency, our dire need of God. We learn not from outside, but from the depths of our own hearts, the meaning of Christ's words: "Without me you can do nothing."

In our tenderness for those whom we love, above all in our love for children, we know God in His image and likeness in ourselves. Knowing Him thus, we cannot fail to trust His tender pity for us.

From coming to know God as our Father through our dependence, and as Father and Mother and Lover through His image in our souls, we learn the simplicity, the humility and trust of children, but only if we dare to love one another —if we accept the loves that come to us in our lives, saying to each one as it comes: "Be it done unto me according to your word," accepting the love and whatever its cost may be, the responsibility of it and the labour, the splendour of it and the sorrow.

As we grow old, we regain our likeness to little children even outwardly. It is in surrendering to this that we make our old age a thing of beauty and peace. We become dependent on others. Our pleasures become fewer and simpler, more and more like those of a child. We let go, at last, of the struggles of the complicated years that are over. The hopes that are no more, the foolish little ambitions, the forgotten griefs. Bereavements cease now to be loss, and change to the anticipation of meeting our living dead again very soon. Our values become true again, we distinguish as unerringly as a child between the essential and the inessential. Our memory goes back to dwell again in the morning of our life. Thus, when death comes, we are able to accept this greatest of all our experiences with a child's capacity for complete experience, and dying we are made new.

There is nothing that is so irksome as the ache of an old wound, and it is from countless old wounds, old sores and weals and suppurating sores and gangrenous wounds that the world is bleeding to death. It is old wounds that are poisoning the life-stream of humanity.

It is no wonder that there has never before been so conscious a longing for a "new Heaven and a new Earth."

Men look more wistfully on the first leaf of Spring than they have ever done before.

To wake one morning to see the first prick of green on a city tree is to experience joy like the receiving of a sacrament.

To look out of the window upon a patch of blue sky newly washed with rain is an experience as poignant and sweet as a sudden vivid memory of childhood, in which for a moment we walk on thinly sandalled feet through the long, dewy grass of a tangled garden that is no more.

So old are we, so old our aching wounds, that loveliness which is actually here and now seems to be a memory. The heart cries out to be made new and to renew the earth.

This is precisely what happens when we become children. We are made new: our newness renews the earth.

We are restored to the sense of wonder. We see the stars,

the coming of Spring, the familiar faces of our friends, the white bread on the table; for the first time we dimly apprehend the mystery of the sacramental quality of the substance of our daily life.

Our values become true. A child does not think or feel in terms of materialism. He does not despair or even worry a little, when the material world collapses.

In little things of no value he receives the Sacrament of the Universe; his jewels are chips of salted and frosted glass that he finds on the sea-shore; he listens for the sound of the sea in a hollow shell, and he hears the song of God.

To become a child is to know with a child's intuition, to see with a child's vision. To see everything with the amazement of seeing for the first time and with the spontaneous giving of the whole heart that is the unique joy of first love. To see human suffering, not with an adult's reasonable despair, but with a child's immediate, unquestioning compassion, that admits no obstacle to its response.

Within our own lifetime we have witnessed a wonder, that of those who are only children in years becoming Christ-children, much more truly children than they were—and these children simply take every small suffering in their lives and offer it to God. They do not question the worth of their immolation, God holds the scales; in one side is their littleness, in the other they put the love of the Infant Jesus.

If anyone becomes a child, that is the Christ-child, or if he only recognizes the presence of the Divine Infant in his life, the sense of futility leaves him.

The Divine Infancy in us is the logical answer to the

peculiar sufferings of our age and the only solution to its problems.

If the Infant Christ is fostered in us, no life is trivial. No life is impotent before suffering, no suffering is too trifling to heal the world, too little to redeem, to be the point at which the world's healing begins.

The way to begin the healing of the wounds of the world is to treasure the Infant Christ in us; to be not the castle but the cradle of Christ, and in rocking that cradle to the rhythm of love, to swing the whole world back into the beat of the Music of Eternal Life.

It is true that the span of an infant's arms is absurdly short; but if they are the arms of the Divine Child, they are as wide as the reach of the arms on the cross; they embrace and support the whole world; their shadow is the noon-day shade for its suffering people; they are the spread wings under which the whole world shall find shelter and rest.

CHAPTER SEVEN:
REDEMPTIVE CHILDHOOD

Meditation on the unity of Christ's life, of how the Passion is in the Infancy and the Infancy in the Passion, proves to us that our own lives need not be lived on an heroic scale to be redeeming. This is of huge significance to us today, faced by appalling suffering all over the world.

In spite of the fact that human nature is weak and selfish and that these faults, crippling as they already are, are aggravated in many today by a positive habit of fear, there can hardly be anyone, excepting the completely dehumanized, who does not long to do something to mitigate the world's sorrow, to ease the suffering of humanity, even if only by the tiniest jot.

It seems that human anguish is a gathering tide, a storm rising higher and higher, sweeping its dark waves wider and wider and closer and closer, and we feel futile, utterly helpless to do anything to stop it. As helpless as if we were literally face to face with an ocean sweeping towards us in a flood of towering waves, and we were told to hold it back with our naked hands.

The magnitude of suffering makes our lives seem even more futile than we have realized before.

What, we ask ourselves, have we ever done to help, say, one persecuted child in the misery of Europe? Of what smallest use to the multitudes of the needy are our lives? Of what use are they at all, to anyone, these little circumscribed lives, consisting of doing the same meaningless things every day, for the same number of monotonous hours, winding up with the same frustrating weariness and drowsiness every night?

We seem useless even to those in our own circle, our family and friends. When one of them meets with real grief, something which drives deep into the soul, we are helpless before it. We can do nothing. More often than not we cannot even find words to express our sympathy, or we are too self-conscious to speak them, and we let the moment in which compassion could have meant so much pass by. Looked at superficially, it seems that every individual must live his life alone, in spiritual isolation, as if we have all, to some extent, made ourselves our prison.

On the material plane, too, we are helpless. Even if we were both millionaires and geniuses, we could not stem even the merely material misery of the world. Money has ceased to be power and, because it was the one power of the materialistic world, that world is tottering. The problems of evil and of misery, interlocked as they are, have gone far beyond what the human mind can solve.

The longing to help humanity, to be in communion with other people, is genuine enough in most of us, but we are frustrated, or imagine ourselves to be, by the smallness and insignificance of our circumstances, by our innate limitations, our lack of skill or talent or opportunity.

Even in something about which everyone must surely agree in his heart, the necessity of avoiding a new war, we feel helpless; evidently fear, though it is strong to destroy and separate, is not strong enough to unite.

The problem is first of all spiritual—or rather, I would say, supernatural. The word "spiritual" is apt to be misunderstood, to be taken to mean bodiless or divorced from the body; our life is sacramental, it is a welding of soul and body. This is one reason why we can never escape the obligation of trying to help one another materially, even when the attempt looks like the folly of Don Quixote tilting at windmills; but our ability to persevere in that depends on our supernatural awareness; unless we see the inward meaning of life, we must despair.

The inward meaning of life is Christ. Our supernatural life *is* Christ. "Without me," He says, "you can do nothing." Our only power to do anything in this world is the power of Christ's love in us.

If we had in fact only our own puny hands with which to beat off and hold back the flood of the world's suffering, then, without question, we should be drowned in it.

The only hands that can hold back that storm are the hands of Christ; and because it is driven and lashed by sin, it is held back only by Christ's hands crucified. Because Christ chose this way to redeem the world—the Way of the Cross—only the hands of Christ on the Cross can control the world's suffering.

In the world, in the human race as a whole, just as in each individual human life, love and death are face to face. Love is Christ on the Cross; facing the world with His arms wide open, His hands nailed back, His heart bare to the lance.

The Word of God is translatable into any language: it is the Word telling the Father's love to men. Whatever suffering any individual anywhere in the world offers up for mankind in the Crucified Christ becomes the word uttered in his native tongue.

All those who have thus offered any suffering for the world are one; they live together, one body in the Crucified Christ.

Christ on the Cross is the oneness of the world. In Him all our individual suffering is integrated in one redeeming act of Love.

In the Crucified Christ the "other Christs" of every nation meet. In Him they are one. They are together and one in the Passion of love that is redeeming the world.

A Christian has no enemies. Those who formerly wounded one another bleed together from the same wounds, the wounds of the Crucified Christ. Poured from His wounds their blood sows the world again with the seed of love. Those who have killed one another in war rise in Him as one, overcoming death, together as one man in Him, with His greeting: "Peace be to you!" on their lips.

This thought makes us more ashamed than ever of the littleness of our lives, of the smallness of our ideal in daily life, of the pettiness of the things that we have supposed to be sufferings: the irksome restraints necessary for peace in family life; the repressions forced upon us if we are to live without bloodshed in lodgings; the slights and humiliations that we sometimes do suffer, and always imagine that we suffer, in the office; the awareness of our own unimportance—how trifling and how ludicrous it all seems after all, and how terrible a failure in us, that we magnify it, when one real stab of suffering, accepted with a whole heart and a willing mind, lifts us up with Christ and with all the suffering humanity in Him, to redeem the world in the very heart of Love!

Yet, after meditating all this on Monday, we are as petty as before on Tuesday.

We must go back to Bethlehem; we have seen that there the Infant Christ was the inscape of Christ on Calvary. That His Passion was in the Suffering of the tiny Child.

It is exactly the same today; if we are baptized, by water, by blood or by desire, the Infant Christ is born in our soul and is our soul's life, and the Passion is lived in the Infant Christ in us.

If the Infant Christ is fostered in us, then, through those sufferings which seem so small because we are so small, we are lifted up with the Crucified Christ.

Suffering does not redeem simply because it is suffering. It does not help those in need more or less because it is greater or less great suffering. Suffering does not necessarily help at all; it does not necessarily unite us to God, in fact it can separate from Him. Suffering can make us bitter, cynical, cruel; it can drive us to despair.

Trivial suffering is not trivial in its effects; it has tremendous power for good and tremendous power for evil; it can be destructive, and warp and starve our personality. It is almost always trivial suffering which, when it is not deliberately sanctified, results in the most lethal disease of the human character, self-pity.

Self-pity reveals a void in us, an emptiness which is the absence of God, a vacuum which sucks us in, into ourselves, distorting us in the process. All our experience is sucked in too, to fester in the vacuum and poison us.

God's presence or absence is known by the effect of suffering on us, especially by the effect of the small sufferings of every day, such as the "slights" which literally corrode those who try to endure them in their own strength. But in those in whom Christ abides, it is Christ who suffers every humiliation; for them there are no psychological scars, the Humility of Christ clothes them in His Majesty and crowns them. Crowns them with thorns, it is true, but what other crown could anyone who thinks wish to wear today? And what other would not be ludicrous?

It is not *what* is suffered that redeems and heals, it is *who* suffers. One tear of Christ's could redeem the world: all the tears of the whole world that are not His are of no avail to comfort one child.

What matters to us is not that we suffer, or that we suffer a little or a lot, but that Christ suffers in us. That Christ suffers whatever we suffer. Not that our lives are small or are lived on an heroic scale, but that they are lived by Christ in us. Therefore, our way to share in the world's healing, to mitigate the world's suffering, is simply to foster and cherish the Infant Christ in our souls.

Because the Christ in us is the Infant Christ, it is in our littleness that we are stretched to the size of the cross; it is in our helplessness that we are crucified in Him.

The Massacre of the Innocents which started in Bethlehem has spread all over the world today. And the Passion of the

Infant Christ which started in Bethlehem is the answer of the saints of our days.

The outward visible resemblance to Bethlehem is not far to seek; it is always the children who are the first victims of tyranny; above all when the Herods of our days want to drive Christ out of a country, it is the children who become their objective. Either they seek to destroy Christ in the children, or to drive the children out; and the former is perhaps the more terrible form of murder, for the attempt is to kill Childhood itself.

The Nativity was the occasion, in a sense the cause, of the murder of a host of little children. That was the immediate result of the Incarnation of Love.

Those little boys were unbaptized Jews. Had they grown to manhood, God alone knows what their individual destinies would have been. But whatever they might have been, they would certainly be long forgotten, they would have no part in us now, no comfort for our sorrow, no redeeming for our sin, no beauty for the lifting of our hearts, no lesson to sustain our hope. Their Eternity would not have been as it is, the purest joy that God, even God, can give, unimaginable, unending delight in Him.

Baptized in blood, those little Jewish children were among the first comers to Heaven. Fittingly they, with their tiny King, are the founders of the Kingdom of Children. We celebrate their Feast with joy, it is the most lyrical in the year. They reach down their small hands to comfort every father or mother bereaved of a child. They are the first who have proved that the Passion of Christ can be lived in a tiny span by little ones. They are the forerunners of the magnificent sanctity of our generation, the "spiritual childhood" of St. Theresa of Lisieux. The tears that dried on their faces two thousand years ago in Jerusalem have the redeeming power of Christ's tears today. Each one of those infants is the first Christ-Child of the Incarnation, the first of the first generation to call the Mother of God blessed—"From henceforth all generations shall call me blessed."

Herod ordered the children to be killed because he was afraid that any one of them might be Christ.

Any Child might be Christ!—the fear of Herod is the fear of every tyrant, the hope of every Christian, and the most significant fact in the modern world.

Any Child might be Christ; yes, and Herod in his attempt to destroy that one Child, to eradicate the threat of the Infant from his nation, baptized a host of children in their own blood and made a legion of little "Christs," who should come unseen with heavenly weapons, flocking to the tattered and blood-soaked standard of innocence through all the ages of mankind.

What processions of little children the Holy Innocents, and with them the Guardian Angels, have followed across the world in our own times, and are following now! From the day when, thirty years ago, Russian children were driven before the Red army, to be tossed alive into open graves in the Steppes, until now.

From Czechoslovakia, France, Belgium, Holland, Java, Korea, Greece, Poland, Estonia, Latvia, Lithuania, Rumania, Bulgaria, Albania, Jugoslavia, Finland, Hungary, Austria, Serbia, Croatia, Slovenia, Bosnia, Montenegro and Macedonia, children have been persecuted and driven out or killed by tyrants, who, whether they bear the name of one ideology or another, can equally be identified with Herod.

Who can doubt that the angels and Innocents meet these little victims of the Godless to speed their way to God?

And on earth, the answer to Herod is still the Incarnation; still the Birth of the Infant Christ, the life of the world in the least and the littlest.

The characteristic of modern sanctity crystallizes the answer of Christ to Herod now. It is the sanctity of spiritual childhood; that sanctity which St. Theresa of Lisieux has defined —holiness that means becoming a child, not just any child, but the Christ-Child.

That which St. Theresa calls her "Little Way" has set fire to and illuminated the world: it has entered into millions of homes. It is a flame of love blown on the great wind of the spirit, but one which has kindled many very humble little fires. It burns in the hearth of poor homes, in the mercy of nightlights in the rooms of sleeping children, in the lamp set for a welcome in the cottage window. It is both the Star of Bethlehem and a candle in the hand of love. The Spirit has borne it and bears it still, not only on the mighty wind, but on the zephyr that carries the warm sunlight and the smell of wild flowers gently through the rooms of the house.

It is the light that illumines where reason stops short, and the breath that blows the smoking flax to flame.

Yet it is a mystery, almost a miracle, that the present-day world should have responded—more, surrendered—to that young French nun. For she is—or rather, seems to be—what most people, and especially most English people, dislike. She was sentimental, so much so that one is forced to ask whether she may be an outlet for the inhibited sentimentality that is a symptom of one of the several epidemic psychological diseases of this age.

The exaggerated repudiation of sentimentality does not cover the depth of feeling that its votaries pretend that it does; on the contrary, it is a pitifully transparent symptom of emotional impotence. Impotence of the deep and tender feeling which not only gives grace and poetry to life but gives balance to the whole personality.

Not only are there many psychologically sick people who can only suffer, and even only love, vicariously through theatres and books, but there are many more who, while repudiating sentimentality with tell-tale violence, will flock to see child prodigies on the screen in order to obtain the faintly sickening solace of tears, produced by synthetic sentimentality.

In many people that sap which drives the tender green shoot into the light and causes the dry wood to blossom has dried up.

Could there be such an explanation for the world-wide acceptance of "The Little Flower of Jesus" and her shower of roses?

I think not; because these roses grow out of the dark and bitter wood of the Cross.

St. Theresa expressed herself in a way which belittled her own greatness. Her constant reiteration of the word "little," her indiscriminate scattering of sugary adjectives all over her autobiography, hides the bones of suffering that she is really speaking about, like a pretty printed cloth thrown over a skeleton.

Consequently many think that her "little way" means her "easy way," and so miss the whole point of her message.

She did not teach the way of Spiritual Childishness, but of Spiritual Childhood. She did not simply become a child, but a Christ-Child, the child of God, whose suffering is the suffering of the Cross, whose love is the love of the Cross.

Her own life was neither easy nor ordinary; it had the quality of iron. She suffered to the limit in mind and body and spirit. She suffered beyond the pitch of human endurance from the exploitation of her unselfishness; she knew as much as that other Carmelite, St. John of the Cross, of the dark night of the soul, and far less of sweetness than he. She knew the desolation of Christ's cry on the Cross—"My God, My God, why hast Thou forsaken Me!"

She did not value her extraordinary sufferings more than her ordinary ones; she estimated the minute irritating things of every day as being of equal value to the tragic things in her life. She knew that the nervous irritability of an exhausted body tortured by the rattling of a rosary in the silence had the same kind of power to redeem as the pains of her death.

No one has ever realized the value of little things as she did; for no one has ever realized more that the Christ-Child suffered in her, and that the Christ-Child can suffer nothing that is not in the redeeming Passion of Infinite Love.

It is this sentimental, passionate little nun, St. Theresa of Lisieux who, in her own life, has defined the sanctity of today, the answer to the Herods of today: it is the sanctity of Spiritual Childhood.

To overcome the world we must become children. To become a child we must fold our consciousness upon the Divine Infant Who is the centre of our being, Who is our being itself; and all that we are must be absorbed in Him, whatever remains of self must be the cradle in which He lies. This is the answer to Herod in our times, the answer of St. Theresa of Lisieux in our times, the "little way of spiritual childhood," which is the oneing of the soul with God, in the Passion of the Infant Christ.

CHAPTER EIGHT:
JUSTICE

ABROAD the Infant Christ is hunted and persecuted. In England He has become a foundling. He who has said to us with such tenderness: "I will not leave you orphans" has been left an orphan in countless souls, where He lives but is forgotten, neglected and even unknown.

There are many of whom this tragic indictment is true and who yet are not culpable for it. The vast number of English people whose Baptism was regarded by their parents as a social occasion, not as a sacrament; whose god-parents were chosen, not for their Faith, but for the material advantages which might result from the compliment paid to them, and who have been brought up "free to choose their own religion," which is to say without any definite teaching about any religion at all, in an atmosphere of shifting prejudice, doubt and materialism, with no example of Christian practice in their homes, and instead of it a general understanding that any outward adherence to God is in bad taste and the whole subject of Faith sufficiently embarrassing to be taboo in polite conversation.

Moreover, they grow up in an environment of materialism by which they are necessarily submitted to the daily suggestion that the only really unimportant things are the things of the spirit.

Attendance at Church is mainly confined to weddings and funerals and occasional national days of prayer; but with the increase of registry office weddings and the lack of immediate danger of invasion, funerals take the lead, so that, to the very people who most fear death and who avoid facing its inevitability, the thought of God becomes associated with the thought of death, and from this it follows naturally that they shrink from the very idea of the personal love of God as a form of morbidity.

What has happened to the little flame of Christ-life that illuminated these souls on the day of their Baptism?

If they have not killed their supernatural life by deliberate sin, Christ remains in their lives, but is orphaned in them. They do not know the wonder of the Motherhood that they have forfeited; if they have any culpability, it is in so far that their souls are too noisy, with the clamour of the fears and desires and pleasures and grievances that they continually entertain, to hear the weeping of the tiny Child in their house.

There is in this one more note in the unity of the Passion and the Infancy. The Divine Child takes upon Himself the characteristic sorrows of the race in which He abides. In His infancy in us, He is identified with the suffering that our sins have inflicted on our children.

Divorce, arrogance and thoughtlessness have given us a nation of spiritually starved children. Over a thousand of them between six and twelve years old, evacuated from London during the War, were questioned concerning their knowledge of God by a group of people temporarily responsible for them; out of them all, one only was familiar with Christ's Holy Name—as a swear word; not one knew that Christ was God, or even who God is.

The Christ-Child in the soul of the average English man or woman is a forgotten, unwanted child, waiting for adoption in a children's "home" that is not a home, for it is without beauty and without love.

"The sins of the fathers are visited upon the children." How true that is and how baffling! It seems the limit of injustice. But, because the sins of the whole race are visited upon the *Christ-Child in us,* whose sorrow redeems, we see that here is the mysterious justice of God which is the logic of extreme love.

Our sins are visited upon our children; but the sorrows of our children are carried in the Divine little hands which, though they have been folded in death, have unfolded and lived to open the buds of two thousand springs with their touch.

Besides those who do not know the mystery of their own being, there are others in whom the Christ-Child needs fostering; people who through circumstances share some essential characteristic of childhood: dependence, poverty, the necessity to obey, and so on.

Very old people and invalids, the nervously unstable, "borderline cases" who are avoided instinctively by happier people. Prisoners, the inmates of workhouses, institutions and asylums. Coloured people segregated by soulless conventions, psychopaths, workers who are subject to the authority of others, conscripts to the Services, sinners who have lost their way like bewildered children lost in a city. And children who are really children in years, but in whom the Divine Child is neglected—spoilt children, nurse-bound children, deliquent children, children without homes.

Besides all these, and many more, there are those who share the outward circumstances of the Infant Christ in Bethlehem, in the desert, in Egypt.

Foreigners, strangers here, who have fled from their own countries, where they were not strangers but of the family and at home. Jews, who have perceived the prophecies in the storm of suffering scattering their race, and by becoming Christians have given birth to the Messiah in Israel. Converts, in whom the Faith is still a new-born, naked Child, blinded by the blaze of the light of glory, and even by the flicker of votive candles!

The Divine Foundling has his foster-parents in the world.

Every mother may contemplate the Infant Christ in her own children. But there is also a vocation of motherhood for the childless. Listen to these mysterious words of Our Lord: ". . . whosoever shall do the will of my Father that is in heaven, he is my brother, and sister, *and mother*." (Matthew xii. 50.)

There are nuns who mother Christ in orphans and in school children; but it is not of these that I am speaking, but of those celibates who seem to have no place or *raison d'être* at all in the eyes of the world, but who, nevertheless, know well the truth of those words: "Many are the children of the barren, more than of her who has a husband."

To be a foster-mother or father of the orphaned Christ is a sublime vocation; it exacts a profound humility from those who are called to it and confers a unique majesty upon them. Very often the worldly, with their ideals of Hollywood, pass such people by with a vaguely uncomfortable contempt; they regard celibacy itself as either a disease or a disgrace and, in either case, a disaster. Lives that are neither those of married people nor vowed religious, which are not breathless with social success or obsessed with making money; lives so "empty" that there is time in them to "go about doing good," as Christ did on earth, lives which are, in fact, spent largely with the lowly and the outcasts and the insignificant seem to the vast masses of mediocracy to be deserts of arid waste, stony uncultivated wildernesses.

But, in the eyes of God, they are the wilderness that flowers. If they are in a wilderness, these foster-parents of the Child Jesus, they are there with the angel who comforted Christ after the forty days of fasting, and with their proto-type St. Joseph with the Infant Christ in the desert:

> Thus saith the Lord: The land that was desolate and impassable shall be glad, and the wilderness shall re-joice and shall flourish like the lily. It shall bud forth and blossom, and shall rejoice with joy and praise: the glory of Libanus is given to it; the beauty of Carmel, and Saron; they shall see the glory of the Lord, and the beauty of our God (Isaias xxxv. 1. *Mass for Satur-day, Ember Week of Advent.*)

These foster-parents of Christ are not those terrible re-formers of individual lives who, urged and driven by an unrecognized sense of power or vanity, interfere with people's lives, fumbling at the locked doors of their souls with clumsy fingers, and bruising when they touch to heal.

They are, on the contrary, sensitive people who approach others, not with exhortation, but with sympathy. Not with self-satisfaction, but with humility.

They give and they listen, they see the spark of life wherever it is and fan it by the warm breath of their humanity; they reverence the solitude of other people's souls; they bear other people's burdens and rejoice in their joy, without imposing upon them. Not only do they tread delicately not to crush the broken reed, but they go down on to their knees to bind it up. They take the neglected Christ-Child to their own hearts instinctively and comfort Him.

They are those people who will be amazed when Christ calls them on the day of Judgment and greets them by telling them that they gave *Him* food and shelter and clothed Him and came to Him in prison. For it is certainly not those who make a double-entry account of their kindness, and have a balance-sheet of "merit" prepared against the day of wrath, who will receive this lovely recognition and be astonished by it:

"Then shall the just answer him, saying: Lord, when did we see thee hungry, and fed thee: thirsty and gave thee drink? And when did we see thee a stranger and took thee in? Or naked and covered thee? Or when did we see thee sick or in prison and came to thee? And the king answering shall say to them: Amen, I say to you, as long as you did it to one of these my least brethren, you did it to me." (Matthew xxv. 37-40.)

They are "the Just," and of St. Joseph, Christ's earthly

Foster-Father, the Evangelists tell us this one thing without elaboration: he was "a just man."

Justice and just people are the world's present crying need. Justice is a word that is on many lips and in few hearts, for it is little understood.

When we say, "I must have justice!" we usually mean, "I must have the relief of hurting as I have been hurt, of despoiling as I have been despoiled."

"Blessed are those who hunger and thirst after Justice" does not mean "Blessed are those who are tormented by a personal grievance against life," or "Blessed are those who, having put themselves in the place of God, have judged others and now itch to see their sentences carried out."

Justice is not vengeance, it is love; in it is included forgiveness; yet there are many who think that forgiveness is *in*justice!

If it were, Christ would not have commanded us to forgive as often as we are injured, or have made that, for each one of us, the condition of our own forgiveness in His day of judgment.

If we knew the heart of man as God knows it, and the network of interdependence which spreads the responsibility for every sin, not only among countless people, but over many generations, we should not attempt to untwist the skeins of right and wrong. For us, justice is to forgive and to make reparation ourselves for all sin.

We must be just, not because we are judges—for that we are not—but because we are trustees of God's love to the world, and justice is a supreme expression of His love. Justice belongs to God, it is a tender expression of His tenderness and pity.

By this word "pity," I do not mean the contemptuous patronage from which sensitive people shrink. Pity is the gentleness of the strong.

It is compassion that identifies the strong with the weak in suffering. It is the skill and gentleness of the strong hand, that lifts without breaking and tends without hurting the open wound. It is the expression of the selfless love that is born of compassion, of the sharing of the sorrow. Love which brings the strong man to his knees to wipe the tears from the face of the tiny child in reverence and awe.

Justice is the defence of the defenceless. It protects the weak, and restores to little ones those things of which they have been robbed by force.

The forgiveness demanded of us by justice means forgiving the injury done to ourselves. We may leave it to others to forgive the injury done to them; this more especially when they are weak and wronged by the strong and powerful; for then the just must come to their defence.

St. Joseph, the "just man" who was Christ's foster-father, is an example of this. The grey-beard statues of him that we are used to, and drugged by, quite misrepresent his character. He was one who did violence to himself, who accepted hardship and danger, and renounced self to protect the little and the weak. In that mysterious anguish of misunderstanding of Our Lady, his one thought in the midst of his own terrible grief was how to save and protect her from the world. It fell to his lot to save the divine Infant from Herod. He, like all those who cherish the life of an infant, had to give up all that he had in order to give himself. We know nothing of him after Christ's boyhood; all that is recorded of him is that he protected Our Lady in Advent, that he was the first to protect the unknown, unguessed Christ in another, and that he was the defence of the Infant Christ when he was defenceless and threatened by Herod. A just man and a strong man. Love was in him like the crystal in the rock. Justice is both the tenderest and the sternest expression of God's Fatherhood: it is the inflexible logic of Divine Love.

It is both the kiss of peace on our mouth and the sword in our hand. It is the sword in the hand of pity.

That which in our eyes seems unjust is often the extreme logic of love which is justice.

It seems unjust to us, when young men in the May-time of their lives, and often the gentlest of them, must go to war and be slain; when the poet must die with the poem still in his heart, the lover with his love still unconsummated.

But it is Christ on the Cross who dies all their deaths. In Him, in the Word of God's love, all poetry is uttered; in Him, Incarnate Love, all love is consummated. On the field of Calvary, the battle between love and death is fought which restores the Kingdom of Heaven to the children whom Satan has despoiled.

Justice is the rich giving to the poor; the strong defending the weak; the injured forgiving the injurer. Calvary was all that. There, Christ was the young man slain, but He was the rich man giving to the poor, Innocence forgiving sinners, the hero restoring the Kingdom of Heaven to the lowly.

Today justice must restore the Kingdom of Heaven to the

little nations. The nations which are little, not in their territory, but in their participation in Childhood.

Sorrowful countries in the power of tyranny, outwardly depersonalized by the pattern of the ideology imposed upon them by force, their own characteristics and racial beauty effaced for the time being, stripped of their national dress, as Christ was stripped of His garments. Poor as children; subject as children; helpless as children.

These little countries are Bethlehems. It is certain, because the conditions of the Incarnation are realized in them, that in them the Incarnation is taking place. In many afflicted lives, clothed in the drab uniformity of the tormentor's bleak mind, Christ is born—"He has no comeliness whereby you shall know him."

God does not change—the Nativity, true to His plan, takes place as it always has, in secrecy, in humility, in darkness.

In that darkness shines the Star of Bethlehem.

Lift up your eyes and see the star, burning over the martyr countries of the world.

We cannot cast off our responsibility to these Bethlehems. We cannot, unless we wish to identify ourselves with Pilate, wash our hands of Czechoslovakia, and Poland.

We cannot, unless we wish to be identified with the crowd that shouts out "Crucify Him," leave Austria, Germany, Hungary to be torn to pieces by men who hate God.

We cannot delude ourselves that time and distance efface the guilt of unexpiated sin.

What doom awaits us if we, who assented to the choice

of Barabbas in Czechoslovakia in 1938, betray the already betrayed Christ again there in 1948?

What doom awaits us if we are among those who have said of Hiroshima and Nagasaki—"Their blood be upon us and upon our children!"

What doom awaits us if we are one of those who insult the face of Poland with the kiss of Judas?

Justice constrains us to insist openly on the rights of the little nations, to do penance for the sins against them in our own lives, to give all that we can for their relief, and to be ready, if it is expedient to do so, to give our lives for the restoring of the freedom of the Divine Child in their midst.

For in them Christ will be born again; that lovely truth which haunts Herod down the ages will be realized—any Child may be Christ. In any humble, frustrated life, Christ may be born. It may be that in the heart of an old peasant, who has lost all his sons, the Divine Son will be born, and the old man will be made new, and his life will renew the earth. It may be that in the life of some forgotten prisoner, the Incarnation will take place, and there, secretly, in swaddling bands, the country's life will begin again. It may be that in the soul of a hungry little child the Light that illuminates the whole world will begin to shine in darkness.

When Christ, born secretly in the little nations, in the martyr countries of the world, is recognized and worshipped openly, those countries will be clothed in their own particular heritage of beauty once more and receive back their own individual character.

Then the meek will inherit the earth, the earth that has nourished them like a mother; that has flowered for them and given them their bread. The earth on which their homes were built; the earth that has been watered with the blood of their sons and in which their sires sleep.

The gentle one, in whose power the meek will inherit the earth, will be the Child-Christ, crowned as King.

Then the bereaved will see the Child King again; and He will have the face of one of their own sons. In Germany He will be a fair boy with wide blue eyes, and suddenly German children will laugh again; in Poland He will be grave but with childhood's gravity, and will turn to the people the face of dusky gold and the damson eyes of their little sons. In France His sceptre will be the crook of the shepherd boys their sons were long ago. In Japan He will walk among the reeds on naked delicate feet, and to every parent the little Child of ivory will come back. In Russia He will come back again among the peasants, the oval of his grave and holy face caressed by the flickering of the ikon lamps.

When the Christ-Child is crowned again in the little nations, then, and only then, there will be Peace on earth:

"And thou, Bethlehem Ephrata, art a little one among the thousands of Juda: out of thee shall he come forth unto me that is to be the ruler in Israel: and his going forth is from the beginning, from the days of eternity. . . . And this man shall be our peace." (Micheas v. 2, 5.)

CHAPTER NINE:
THE CHRIST-CHILD'S MOTHER

W HEN the Christ-Child once more reigns, His throne will be His mother's arms.

When He is crowned—as one day He will be crowned—as King of the Jews in Palestine, He will rule from the arms of Our Lady of Mount Carmel. In Czechoslovakia, in a golden cope stiff with gems, from the arms of Our Lady of Prague. In Russia He will lean from the breast of the tenderest of mothers, Our Lady of Vladimir. In England He will be enthroned, firm and merry, on the knee of Our Lady of Walsingham.

It is small wonder that in an age which is the age of Redeeming Childhood, Our Lady is dawning on human consciousness and becoming more and more loved all over the world. For there is no one else who can teach us as she can how to foster the Infant Christ in our lives.

There are many ways in which we can know and think of Our Lady and learn from her. We can think of her as the human mother of the human Christ, and as the model of all human mothers in their relationship to their children. The life of every child's soul is Christ's life; because this is so, every child is *"alter Christus"*—"another Christ"—not in the same sense as the priest, but in a real sense for all that. Every natural mother has literally to take the place of Our Lady, to be a mother of Christ in being a mother to her own child.

Our Lady is also the mother of the human race. Our Lord made her that when He took His human nature from her and made His own life the supernatural life of all men. All Christians, as "Christs," are the children of the Mother of Christ. Our Lady loves each one of us as she loves Christ, as her only child. We actually have a mother in Heaven who is as deeply concerned with us, and with every detail in our lives, as she was with Christ's life on earth.

Another way to think of Our Lady is as the model of those who have no natural children of their own, but who are mothers of the Christ in their own souls. What is said of her in her relationship with Christ on earth applies equally to these other motherhoods of hers, other and yet the same. There is no better way for those who mother the Christ in their souls, who are the mothers of Christ in their supernatural life, than Our Lady's way with Christ in her natural motherhood, just as there is no better and no other way that leads to happiness for natural mothers with their children; and Our Lady's motherhood of the human race is so interwoven with her motherhood of Christ as to be inseparable from it.

For the sake of clarity we try to think of these three aspects of Our Lady's motherhood separately, but of necessity they merge into one another.

Every mother can contemplate Christ in her own child of flesh and blood; but it must be a deliberate contemplation, accepting all the stern, as well as the beautiful and consoling, facts that are implied in it.

There are few platitudes so silly and so harmful as that which declares that the mere biological fact of motherhood is "sacred," and that a mother's love is, *ipso facto*, holy, pure, and selfless.

If any of this were true, then we ought to put a halo round the dear rough heads of the cows in the fields, and the little round heads of the humble cats in the house, for they are truer to nature in their motherhood, and in this respect better mothers, than many of the over-civilized human beings of today.

Human motherhood *can* be the holiest of loves; but it can also be the most unholy. It is capable of a degree of selfishness that is incalculably cruel and destructive, that is too often camouflaged by a thick fog of conventional sentimentalities.

Motherhood is safe only when it is sanctified. We have emotions and problems and fears which animals have not; in us, natural love cannot be separated from supernatural love without disaster.

In this Our Lady is obviously our guide.

When we consider the hardship and danger attending Christ's infancy, the exile in a strange country with all that it involved in the loss of home and of Joseph's trade, it seems remarkable that Our Lady, who was hardly more than a child, could face such trials and bring up an Infant Son in the midst of them.

Until Christ's birth her life had been a sheltered one, far more so than the life of any modern girl. How then had she been prepared?

Her preparation for her maternity was the love of God. The first thing we realize about Our Lady is her deep and exultant love of God. She knew Him through her own prayer and through the Scriptures. It was no fierce tribal god that the little girl in Nazareth discovered in her studies and her meditations. It was the Eternal loving Father, whose first known utterance was "Let there be light!" and whose light shone in her own mind, illuminating it. She knew God as Mother too. For in God there is both Father and Mother. Long years before Christ's revelation in His human life on earth, mystics discovered and prayed to the Mother in God.

In the fifth century B.C. the Chinese teacher Laotse, a contemporary of Confucius, said of God:

"The spirit that can be uttered is not the eternal spirit.

"The name that can be named is not the eternal Name.

"Nameless—He is the origin of heaven and earth.

"Named—He becomes the mother of all beings."

And in India Vivekananda, quoting and commenting on Ramakrishna, said:

> Perfect love is reached by the following stages: Man worships in reverence and asks God's help. He beholds God as His father. He beholds Him as his Mother with an infinite affection and without fear. He loves God for love's sake beyond the Law. He experiences the love of union. This is the higher stage when a man loves God as his Father and his Mother.*

* These passages are quoted in Otto Karrer: *The Religions of Mankind*, pages 38 and 32.

They made their discovery through the blind hands of love reaching out of darkness, and through the likeness of their Creator in themselves, manifest in their tenderest and strongest emotions.

How much more would Our Lady have known the Mother in God through love and through herself? She who was created and designed for one sole purpose: to be the Mother of God—the Mother of Motherhood. If she knew God before she had conceived her Son, how much more intimately she knew Him afterwards, when the Holy Spirit had descended on her.

Then all the light of the Spirit of Love burnt its radiant fires within her, and all the gifts of the Holy Spirit, beginning with Wisdom and Understanding, were given to her to spend on her Child.

For every mother the knowledge of God is the essential preparation for motherhood. To know Him as a tender but infinitely powerful father: then to pray for the descent of the Spirit, for the Divine ray that illumines natural love and bestows all the qualities of the Spirit's indwelling presence, which are the basic necessities in bringing up a child.

Our Lady knew that her child was the Child of God before He was her child, and because she loved God, knowing His goodness, His Fatherhood and His Motherhood, His tenderness and His power, His pity and His justice, above all His love for His children, she was consoled by this knowledge. It made it possible to bear the foreboding of suffering that haunted her. It would have been unbearable to hold that Infant Son in her arms, knowing that He must go away to a life of suffering and a cruel death, were it not for her faith in His Heavenly Father; were it not for her certainty that the hands of God would always be holding Him, and that God's hands, incredible though it seemed, would hold Him even more tenderly, even more securely, than hers.

This knowledge is the necessity for every mother's peace.

What woman, capable of taking thought, could hold her infant in her arms today without foreboding? Every child who is born must bear the suffering that sin has brought into the world, in the measure of his own capacity; and here is a truth that will demand all the courage that nature and grace can muster to face: the more Christ "is formed" in the child, the more he will suffer. Those in whom self predominates *seem* to suffer much; for they make everyone around them continuously aware of everything that they are enduring, either by incessant self-pity and complaints, or by incessant bravado and boasting about their fortitude. But the fact is, the heart concentrated on self contracts; it dries up and shrinks and goes hard like a nut withered inside its husk, and nothing can get through the hardness of its littleness. Its suffering (like the nut's, if that could suffer) is simply its own bitterness, and even that limited to the size of its littleness. But those who are Christo-centric, in whom Christ waxes strong, expand and are wide open to the grief of the world. They are wide as the arms of the Crucified are wide, and their hearts, unable to contain the world's suffering in themselves, break open, as Christ's did, and let the torrent of His pity sweep through them.

Every child who comes into this world comes into it to be a Christ to it. He comes into it to share in the redeeming of it. To take his full share in its work, to carry his full load of its burden of suffering. To help in its healing; to participate in its joy; above all, he comes into it to enter into communion with all other men in it, through love.

If a human creature grows to his full stature of Christhood, then he will most inevitably experience those things which Christ did in His earthly life.

Christ was racked with temptation. He was poor—even, ultimately, homeless and destitute. He was without recognition among His own people. He was misunderstood, and just not understood, by His chosen friends; deliberately misunderstood and misrepresented by His enemies. By those whom He healed He was treated with ingratitude. By those whom He loved He was forsaken in His hour of greatest need, He was denied by His friend. By one of His own, He was sold for a paltry sum of money—a *paltry* sum, just as it is today, when the characteristic of avarice is to destroy sensitive holy things and people for *trifling* sums of money.

To such sorrows as these the Christ-children of the world are born.

Such a destiny for her child could be tolerable to a mother on one condition, and one only, that she herself loved mankind with a passion of love. This Our Lady did.

To her, Christ was not only her Child, not only God's Child even. He was also the Saviour of mankind. He had come into the world to redeem it, and this *because* He was God's Son; for God Himself loves the world, and Christ, His only Son, is His Word, uttering His love: "For God so loved the world as to give his only begotten Son, so that whosoever believeth in him may not perish, but may have life everlasting."

In the *Magnificat,* the cry of Joy wrung from her heart in Advent, Our Lady sings the immortal song of her twofold love: the love of God and the love of man. These two loves became one in her love of Christ, who was both God and Man.

Every suffering, every apparent failure, every frustration in a Christ-child's life, is a fulfilment; a fulfilment of his Christhood, of Christ's life given to the world at his hands.

His Christhood does not mean simply and only that he will suffer. It means that whatever he does suffer will be linked with Christ's suffering and His power of redeeming; and this whatever it is, from a child's first fall on the gravel path or first homesickness at school, to the soldier's death on the battlefield, should that be asked.

His Christhood will not work itself out in his life according to his own plan, or to his mother's plan for him, simply because, though by our reckoning there are two thousand years between Gethsemane and today, in God there is no time, and the life of the "other Christ" in the world today, which seems so different even from the *immolation* he would like to make, is not something gone awry, it is the answer to Christ's prayer in His agony: "Not My Will, but Thine be done."

Christ in His Infancy asks no gift but self from those who love Him. But God does not ask love from His creatures greater than the love He gives to them. On the Cross Christ Himself was stripped of everything but Himself. In the Sacrifice of Himself He gave *Himself* to God and to Man.

Just as the mother who is wise knows that if Christ waxes strong in her child, he will go out to meet suffering half way, and *will* meet it, but his suffering will redeem and comfort and heal, those who foster the Infant Christ inwardly in the life of their soul know that the same applies to them.

Christ, wherever He is, in whomever He is, must be about His Father's business.

It is the favourite accusation of those who, for reasons of their own, are made uneasy by the sight of someone else's honest attempt to practise Faith, that to save one's own soul is a selfish, egocentric pre-occupation which makes one introverted, censorious and withdrawn from other people.

In reality the opposite is true. As Christ grows in the soul, suffering and the capacity for suffering increase in the life, and with it the *desire* to suffer grows, not because of any morbidity, such as masochism, but because if Christ increases, love increases; when the love of God increases, the desire to atone for sin increases, because the lover of God wishes to offer Him a shadowless world; and the desire to suffer for sin increases because the lover of man wishes to heal the wounds from which mankind is bleeding to death.

The Christ-child, knowing himself far short of sanctity, echoes, at least in desire, the words of Christ: "And for them do I sanctify myself." (John xvii. 19.)

The consolation of Our Lady's Motherhood went even beyond the fact that her Son would redeem the world. He would not only heal and comfort sorrow; He would give joy.

Christ brought no sorrow into the world; He brought all its joy. He wed sorrow to Himself, so that even out of sorrow joy is born.

At the Wedding Feast of Cana, because Our Lady pleaded,

the First Miracle was worked. It was a miracle to increase joy. It had nothing to do with sickness or blindness or satanic possession, or even with forgiveness; it was simply done to make those who were happy more happy, and it was a symbol of the Incarnation: the changing of Water into Wine.

What a symbol of the Virgin Mother of God that pure water is. Water is of all things the most selfless, yet without it nothing has life. It irrigates the earth, it gives the spring its tender greenness, it is the life of the flowers and their loveliness, it quenches thirst, it purifies all that it touches. It is the perfection of poverty, it has nothing of its own, it has no shape or colour or taste or radiance; yet it gives unceasingly to all living things and all beauty is perceived in it. In it we see the blue sky and the green leaves and the passing clouds; in it we look with naked eyes upon the moon and the stars and the sun.

As the selfless water at Cana was given up to Christ and was changed to wine by His coming, the selfless virginity of Mary was given up to Him, and in her the tasteless, colourless, shapeless water of human nature was changed to wine—the wine of Christ, alive and life-giving.

There can be no doubt that on the night before He suffered, when He sat among His Apostles eating the Paschal supper with them for the last time, Christ's mind dwelt on that memory of the Wedding Feast at Cana. As He looked down at the flowing red wine circled in the little cup, the wine that He was even now changing into His own Blood, into His life to give the world life, He must have thought of the wine drawn at the end of that other feast, and perhaps the words of the steward echoed in His mind: "But thou hast kept the good wine until now!"

This was the good wine that was to give joy to the world for ever and ever. It was His life-blood, and it was the blood given to Him by Mary, who had said to Him: "They have no wine" at the Marriage Feast.

This was the eve of another wedding, the wedding between love and death. Tomorrow that conflict that is fought out in the life of every infant, and at the birth of the Christ-life in every soul, was to be fought out once and for all on Calvary, and Love would conquer death, not by destroying it, but by embracing it, by taking it to His heart.

This, then, was the joy and strength of the Mother of the Infant Christ. That Christ should redeem, that Christ should heal, that Christ should give joy, that Christ should enter into communion with men and should abide in all men and be their life for ever.

Dying on the Cross, Christ said to His Mother: "Woman, behold your son!" He meant her to see Himself in St. John; but in this He included, not only St. John, but all men.

It was not only in that moment that Mary was to behold her Son: she was to see Him in all men, through all time.

Almost at once, when Christ had said to her: "Woman, behold your son!" He was taken down from the Cross dead and laid in her arms, and she looked at His dead face, swollen, bruised, cut open by thorns, grimed with sweat and dirt and man's spitting. "Woman, behold your son!"

She looked on the face of her Son in all those children of God in whom Christ is dead, in all time.

She saw the face of the sullen adolescent child, whose

mother looks on it today in bewilderment, and she loved it.

She saw the face of the criminal in the dock, whose mother looks on in misery from the well of the Court, and she loved it.

She saw the face of inaccessible loneliness of the delinquent child, and she loved it.

She saw the face of the dissolute, the degenerate, the outcast, that was loved only by the mother who is dead, and she loved it.

She looked upon the face of Him who "Himself without sin, God has made sin for us." And she saw the face of all sinners, through all time, in the face of her dead Child.

Since that hour there is no face of a sinful child of God that is not gazed on from Heaven with eyes of illimitable compassion.

Because Christ is dead in them, the Mother of Christ recognizes the face that she bathed and anointed; the eyes that she closed on Calvary.

"Woman, behold your son!"

Mother of God, we lay our dead Christs in your arms; we lay our dead Christs on your heart!

It is often said that a mother's love for her child can never fail, she will never forsake him and never despair of him. This is not true. It is true that normally the mother's love will be the last to fail, the last to despair. But it has its limitations, beyond a certain point even the deepest natural love cannot go. But the love of the Mother of Christ for every Christ-child who comes into the world cannot fail, cannot despair.

When Our Lady sees the dead Christ whom she laid in

the tomb in the soul of one of God's children today, she sees beyond the tomb to the Risen Christ. She sees exactly the same wounds, the wounds inflicted by sin, but she sees them as the glory of the human race, blazing like stars from the risen hands and feet and heart of her Son. She is the Mother of the Risen Christ. The earthly mother, too, who sees not simply her child, but Christ in her child, who is able to bear his suffering because she knows that it is Christ's suffering, cannot despair for the child, because she knows that if Christ is dead in him, Christ can rise from the dead. Even the wounds that his sins have scored on him, the shame, the disillusionment, the humiliation, the destitution, the loneliness, can turn to his glory. Like Christ he must make his journey into the darkness, into the tomb of sorrow for sin; but like Christ he can come back into the light, risen from the dead, and in the Risen Christ the child will come back.

The Child never died in Christ. All through His Manhood He kept the essential qualities of His Childhood: the capacity for complete joy and complete sorrow; the Child's simplicity; the Child's love of the Father.

To every sorrow that He met in some other person's life, He responded with the unqualified sympathy that only children give. He approached people as children do, asking for a drink of water, wanting nothing but to be loved. Above all, He kept the joy of a child, the child's delight in the loveliness of the earth, in the wide golden harvests, the wild flowers, the birds. His values did not change when He grew up. He liked what was lovely because it was lovely, not because it was valuable. When he wanted to describe something utterly beautiful, He described the grass, so little treasured by men that they burn it in the oven. When He had to produce money to pay a tax, He worked a miracle that is like a fairy story, a miracle that a boy would like to work. Instead of simply calling the money out of the air, He made His apostles find it inside a fish.

He was the Child of God in Bethlehem and the Child of God on the Cross. Never has there been such a cry of a child in the dark as His "My God, my God, why hast Thou forsaken me?" And never such a child's trust falling asleep on the Father's heart as His "Father, into Thy hands I commend my spirit."

When He was taken down from the Cross and laid in His Mother's arms, she knew, just as she knew when she rocked Him to sleep in His infancy, that He was in the hands of God; that God had not suffered a bone in His body to be broken; those bones which had been such a birdlike filigree that she had marvelled that her own gentle touch did not crush them.

He was in the hands of God, resting in Him, and the Father resting in the Son, in the bliss of Their consummated love, as They had rested in one another on the morning of creation.

They rested then, waiting for the Star of Bethlehem and the Infant's waking upon the midnight of Incarnation. Now they rested, waiting for the morning star and the waking of the Risen Christ, in the daybreak of the Resurrection.

God's plan for the Infant Christ was not Our Lady's plan for Him. What good and lovely things she had to give up in order that His will should be done in her, not hers in Him.

In order that what she gave to Him should be *herself!*

She had made the home in Nazareth ready for Him. In her mind for the nine longing months of Advent it had been *His* home.

Joseph had made the wooden cradle and had arranged sufficient work for the lovely months ahead. Mary had woven the blankets for the cradle and clothes for the Child. The lamp that was to burn in the darkness to light the Light of the world was set in its place.

Everything in the plan was good and must surely be pleasing to God.

Yet God altered everything! They were not to go back to Nazareth until the Child had outgrown His cradle and His first clothes. They were not to enjoy the privacy of four walls of their own; they were not to be restricted to the society of the few neighbours in the hamlet; they were not to have the security of Joseph's steady trade.

From the stable in Bethlehem they were to fly into the desert and into Egypt, there to live as foreigners and exiles among a people who were strange to them and to whom they were strange.

This happens so often, too, to those who foster the Infant Christ in their souls. We like to plan the life that we shall offer to God in just the way that seems good and aesthetically right to us, to achieve holiness between four walls, with every modern convenience; besides undisturbed sessions of solitude, work and prayer, and a selected number of friends on whom to exercise our charity and with whom to live, reasonably, easily, at peace.

It is difficult to imagine that a plan like this—so full of

sweet order and prudence and commonsense, so harmless—could not be pleasing to God.

Yet God changes everything.

He sends us to where *He* wants to be; among those whom *He* wishes to be among; to do that which *He* wishes to do in our lives.

He brings to the Bethlehem of our lives those people to whom He wishes to show the Infant Christ in us; those who are to give us something for Him, just as He brought whom He would to Bethlehem: animals, angels, shepherds and kings. Unlikely people, proving that, though there are distinctions between different kinds of men in the world, when they come into Christ's presence there is to be no distinction, no selection; the rich and the poor, the ignorant and the learned, the labourer and the king must kneel together to the Infant Christ.

With all the ingenuity and all the sincerity in the world we cannot arrange our lives as God can to ensure that we give the Infant Jesus *His* necessity in us, not our goods or our thoughts of Him, but ourselves.

Our humanity is to clothe Him. Our love to be the four walls that shelter Him. Our life to sustain Him.

Our prayer must be Our Lady's prayer: "Be it done to me according to thy word!"

He took her at her word, and they fled into the desert. She herself was His food, His warmth, His shade, His home, His cradle and His rest.

CHAPTER TEN:
THE HOST LIFE

IT WOULD SEEM impossible, did we not know it to be true, that God could abide with us always, in littleness and humility even more extreme than infancy. Or that His love should choose to give us the unity of His birth and death and resurrection, always taking place at the heart of the world, from sunrise to sunset, and all life, and all love, always radiating from it.

Yet this is so. Every day, every hour, Christ is born on the altar in the hands of the priest. Christ is lifted up and sacrificed; Christ is buried in the tomb of the human heart and Christ rises from the tomb to be the life of the world through His Communion with men.

This is the Host-life. Everything that has been said in this book could be said again of the Host. Everything relates to the Host.

If we live the Host-life in Christ, we shall bring to life the contemplation of the Passion of the Infant Christ and live it in our own lives.

The Host is the Bread of Life. It is the good seed that the

Sower sowed in His field; it is the Harvest ready for the reaping.

It is the seed that is sown by the Spirit in every public way and every secret place on earth. It is the seed which, whenever it is buried, springs up from the grave, to flower with Everlasting Life.

It is the mystery of the Snowflake. The Inscape of Thabor and of the Passion of the Infant. It is the whiteness, the roundness, the littleness, which at once conceals and reveals the plan of Eternal Love.

It is the littleness, the dependence, the trust in human creatures of the Divine Infancy. It is the silence of the Child in the womb: the constriction of the swaddling bands.

It is the Bread which is broken and yet is our wholeness. The wholeness of all that is. It is the breaking of the Bread which is the Communion of all men in Christ, in which the multiple lives of the world are one Christ-life, the fragmentary sorrows of the world are one Christ-Passion; the broken loves of the world are one Christ-love.

The Host seems to be divided among us; but in reality we, who were divided, are made one in the Host.

It is the obedience of childhood. The simplicity which is the singleness of childhood's love. It is the newness in which Heaven and earth are made new.

It is the birth of Christ in the nations; the restoring of the Christ-Child to the world; of childhood to the children.

With the dawning of this turbulent twentieth century came the children's Pope, Pius X, to give Holy Communion to the little ones. In the hearts of the little children, Christ went out to meet Herod all over the world.

The Mass is the Birth and Death and Resurrection of Christ: in it is the complete surrender of those who love God.

The Miracle of Cana takes place. The water of humanity is mixed into the wine and is lost in it. The wine is changed into the Blood of Christ.

In the offering of the bread and wine we give material things, as Our Lady gave her humanity, to be changed into Christ. At the words of Consecration the bread and wine are not there any more; they simply *are not* any more but, instead, Christ is there.

In that which looks and tastes and feels like unleavened bread, Christ comes closer to us even than the infant could come, even than the child in the womb. He is our food, our life.

We give ourselves up to Him. He gives Himself up to us.

He is lifted up in the priest's hands, sacrificed. God accepts the sacrifice and gives Christ back to us. He is lowered onto the altar; He who was taken down from the Cross is given to us in Communion; buried, laid to rest in our hearts.

It is His will to rise from the dead in our lives and to come back to the world in His risen Host-life.

In His risen life on earth Christ often made Himself recognized only by the characteristic of His unmistakable love; by showing His wounds, by His infinite courtesy, by the breaking of Bread. He would not allow the sensible beauty and dearness of His human personality, His familiar appearance, to hide the essential *Self* that He had come back to give.

Wholly consistent with this is Christ's return to us in the Host. We know that in It He is wholly present, Body,

Blood, Soul, Divinity. But all this is hidden, even His human appearance is hidden. He insists, because this is the way of absolute love, on coming to us stripped of everything but Himself.

For this Self-giving Christ in the Host is poor, poorer than He was when, stripped of everything, He was naked on the Cross. He has given up even the appearance of His body, the sound of His voice, His power of mobility. He has divested Himself of colour and weight and taste. He has made Himself as close to nothing as He could be, while still being accessible to us.

In the Host He is the endless "Consummatum est" of the Passion of the Infant Christ.

In the Host He is our Life on earth today.

There is no necessity for me to describe the average life. Too many know it. Countless millions have to make the way of the Cross and the way to Heaven through the same few streets, among the same tiny circle of people; through the same returning monotony; while many, many others have even less variety in their lives, less outward interest and less chance of active mercy or apostleship—those who are incurably ill or in prison, or very old, confined not only to one town or village, but to one room, to one bed in a ward, to one narrow cell.

Everyone wants to take part in the healing and comforting of the world, but most people are dogged by the sense of their own futility.

Even the power of genius and exceptional opportunity dwindles, measured against the suffering of our times. It is then hardly to be wondered at if the average person whose life is limited by narrow circumstances and personal limitations feels discouragement that is almost despair.

Living the Christ-life means that we are given the power of Christ's love. We are not only trustees of God's love for man, entrusted to give it out second-hand, but miraculously, *our* love IS His love!

"I have bestowed my love upon you, just as my father has bestowed his love upon me; live on, then, in my love." (John xv. 9.)

The Host-life is an intense concentration of this power of love.

The Host-life is not something new or different from the Christ-life that we know already. It is the very core of it, and it was given to us at the Last Supper when Christ gave Himself to us in the Blessed Sacrament.

The Host-life is the life which Christ Himself is living in the world now. It is His choice of how to live His life among us today. At first sight it is baffling that it should be so.

Have *you* never stood before the tabernacle and asked yourself: "Why is He silent, while the world rocks with blasphemies and lies?" "Why is He passive while His followers are persecuted and innocent people are crushed?"

It is almost frightening to seek an answer to the question: "Why does God remain in our midst silent and passive, knowing and seeing everything, but saying and doing nothing, while cruelty, injustice, ignorance and misery go on and on and on?"

It is a frightening question until we remember what it is which alone *can* restore humanity to happiness; that it is one thing only that can do it, namely supernatural life, beginning secretly in each individual heart; just as Incarnate Love began secretly on earth in the heart of Mary. It is one thing only, the birth of the Infant Christ in us, Incarnate Love.

No voice of warning could effect this. That could make men tremble; it could not make them love. No armed force could do it, not even supernatural force. That could make men slaves; love is always free.

Love must begin from within. It must be sown in the inmost darkness of the human heart, and take root and flower from the dust that man is.

This can only happen if the Holy Spirit descends from Heaven and penetrates human nature, as the rays of the sun and summer rain come down into the earth, warming and irrigating the seed that is sown there and quickening it.

Christ sowed the seed of His life in us when He sowed the world with the drops of His Blood from the Cross. Now it is Christ in the Host who draws down the Holy Spirit. For the Holy Spirit is the Eternal Love between the Father and the Son. Love which cannot resist the plea of the silence, the patience, the obedience of the Sacred Host.

In the Host Christ gives Himself to live the ordinary life as it is today, to live it fully in all its essentials, and to take into Himself, into His own living of the Host-life, the most ordinary, the most numerous, seemingly the most mediocre lives, bestowing upon them His own power to bring down the Spirit of Love.

In those who have received Him in Holy Communion Christ goes among whom He will, to whatever places He chooses to be in: with little children He goes into the schoolroom; with office-workers to the office; with shop-assistants to the shop. Everyone with whom the communicant has even a passing contact during the day is someone whom Christ wished to meet. Not only priests, but doctors and nurses and the servants and paper-sellers in hospitals take Him to the sick and the dying: to patients who have forgotten God. Not only the military chaplain, but common soldiers take Him into the barracks and into battle. In their comrades Christ marches side by side with boys who have never been told about His love. He walks in their footsteps.

An unknown martyr priest of our own times, whose anointed hands had been cut off by his persecutors, so that he might never again consecrate bread and wine, sent this message secretly from his exile, asking his friends to take it from one to another round the world:

"I can never again carry the Sacred Host or lift It up in my hands, but no one can prevent me from carrying Our Lord in my heart wherever I am. You, who are not prisoners, who are not held in one place, go often to Holy Communion. Carry Christ everywhere in your hearts. Make your souls monstrances, and go into those places where Our Lord has never been adored in the Host, where the monstrance has never been lifted up."

How often we think that but for this or that person in our lives we should be saints! That troublesome person in the office; that exasperating fellow lodger; that spiteful old relative who is on our back like the old man of the sea! They are our stumbling blocks. Why is it allowed? Why is it that we cannot get away from them?

It is because Christ wishes to be with them and has chosen us to take Him to them. He loves them; He sees the depths of their loneliness: He has plumbed it with His love. *Moreover He approaches us in them.* They bring Him to us in just that aspect that He wishes to be known to us. His presence in them may save us from some particular sin. They may be to us Christ forgiving, Christ in His patience, Christ teaching. They may be Christ in His weariness, or Christ in His fear in Gethsemane, Christ facing His death. They may come dependent and helpless as Christ in His childhood or infancy. They may come as Christ in that particular need of His to which our response means our salvation. Possibly the neglected Christ in the tabernacle to whom we have made such fervent promises of reparation, such acts of self-dedication, still awaits our rudimentary courtesy—unrecognized, unloved and lonely under our own roof.

It takes our breath away to think of Christ's self-giving in the Host. We hardly realize it, because it is so amazing that to speak realistically of it demands a daring that sounds like blasphemy to our unaccustomed ears.

In the Host Christ is silent—in fact voiceless, dependent, even helpless. He is carried in the hands of men wherever they choose. His obedience is beyond death.

Think how aptly countless lives approximate to the Host. In His silence how many there are who must endure in silence; who, sometimes in tragic circumstances, have no opportunity to plead their case. How many, too, are silent through fear. Fear that a complaint may cost them a detested but necessary job. Fear of ridicule, like new children at boarding-school, or boys and girls in the throes of first love. How many there are who are dumb-hearted, inarticulate, unable to express themselves, or who, though they long to unburden their minds to a fellow-creature, never find a willing and sympathetic listener. And there is the religious silence, the "Great Silence" of religious houses, in which men and women bring their whole will to entering into the silence of the Host.

In His dependence and helplessness, surely everyone, at the beginning and end of life, is included. Children, and old people in their last illness; and on any given day, since the supernatural life must be lived out fully *every* day, all those filling the crowded hospitals of the world.

In His obedience; there are vast numbers of people who are subject to others—workers, soldiers, sailors and airmen. Hospital nurses, inmates of institutions, prisoners, children. With few exceptions, everyone.

In the light of the Host-life, shining upon the modern world, it becomes clearly visible that the power of love, of comforting, of healing and alleviating suffering is given to the most unlikely people; to those who seem to be the most restricted; that the most effective action belongs to those who seem helpless and unable to do anything at all, and that there is a tremendous force of contemplation, unrecognized but redeeming, in the midst of the secular world.

But it would be presumptuous to suppose that the mere fact of narrow, limiting circumstances is all that is required. No one is excluded from this contemplation in action. The genius as well as the simpleton can enter into the Host-life, because it does not depend first of all upon outward things, but upon interior things.

The condition on our side is surrender as complete as that which we learn from the service of the Divine Infant: unreserved surrender of self to the life of Christ in the Host. Surrender to Christ as complete as His surrender to us in the Host-life.

It is seldom, when *much* is asked for, that human nature fails to respond. It is when too little (as we think) is asked of us, when we have little to offer, that we fail.

When the offering seems too slight or too fragmentary; something absurd in the face of the Eternal Love that consecrates it, and the immensity of the human suffering that needs it.

In every normal lifetime certain days stand out when some crisis—such as acute pain or danger—integrates, points and concentrates the offering of self; when, momentarily, human nature is vested in a little majesty, and so the idea of immolation seems less absurd. But in the ordinary way it seems futile.

In spite of the heaviness with which they afflict us personally, we have, after all, such trifles to offer: boredom, hurt vanity, uncongenial environment, self-consciousness, little aches and pains, trifling disappointments, brief embarrassments, half-imaginary fears and anxieties. We can hardly believe that God accepts these!

Christ has forestalled all that. The offering to be changed into His Flesh is the most fragile wafer of unleavened bread, light as the petal of a rose; flexible, colourless, only just substance at all. It is made out of tiny separate grains. It is *this* that Christ chooses for His supreme miracle of love. Moreover, He chooses that it shall be offered every day anew. That every day this offering shall be changed into His Body.

We are asked to offer only what we have, what we are today. That it is so little means nothing: it is our wafer of unleavened bread.

If we are troubled by the fact that we are not at one with ourselves, that we are full of conflict and distraction, that we have not even achieved singleness of heart sufficient for one perfect prayer, that we are broken up by distractions, by scattered thoughts, emotions, desires, we must realize that our offering, too, begins by being many separate grains.

We must take one grain, the nearest at hand; a momentary joy, a particular anxiety, a slight discomfort, an aching limb, an embarrassment, and offer that. But in order to offer that, our whole self must be gathered in, integrated in the offering. The offering cannot possibly be made otherwise.

We must bring our minds to it, our will, our heart. We must close our thoughts round it, at least for a second in a shining circle. Thus the offering itself integrates us: in it the scattered grains of our life become one bread.

Imitating Christ in the Host literally, we must make our offering daily, not grieving at the failure of yesterday, but through the offering of today being made new today, and this *every* day.

The Host is Rest. Still, infinite Peace. In this rest is the mysterious activity of Love. It is the rest of the love between the Persons of the Blessed Trinity.

It is the rest of Christ on earth.

It is Christ's rest in Advent: the silence, the dependence, the secrecy of the unborn. In the Host-life men contribute to this rest by giving themselves to be Himself, as Our Lady gave herself. It is the rest of surrender.

It is Christ's rest by the well, when He asked the woman of Samaria for a drink of water. The rest of the Human Christ, who allows Himself to be tired for our sake and asks for refreshment. It is the rest that asks for reparation, for the cup of cold water, for which Christ will give back the living water of immortality. It is the rest of the Humility which allowed the woman—a sinful woman at that—to achieve, through His weariness, what He Himself did not achieve through His power: the conversion of a whole village.

It is the rest of Christ sleeping in the boat, while the storm terrified His Apostles. The Faith which enables the children of God to sleep on His heart while the storm of evil and suffering rocks the world around them.

It is the rest of Christ in the tomb, the profound rest of Communion, when Christ is laid in the human heart and asks of those who receive Him there Silence, Darkness, Death. Silence, which is the stillness of the heart at Holy Communion, not broken by fear or thought or wilfulness: the wordless silence of trust. The Silence of the trust in the Father into whose hands we commit not only *our* little life, comparable to a sparrow's life and the life of grass, but the Real Life, Christ in us, our Being. The Silence of the lips closed upon the *"Consummatum est!"*

The Darkness is the darkness of Faith which is content to see nothing, to feel nothing; the darkness and obliteration of the senses, the Faith which asks for no reassurance, no sign of the Divine Presence, no stir of life in the sown field. The Faith which accepts the appearances in which the Divine life is concealed in the Host as its own soul's portion, and is content without colour or odour or sound or taste.

The Death is the death of self. In this death the life of self which is the life of corruption, the restlessness of the worms in a corpse, ceases in silence and darkness: in this death is peace: like the peace which embalmed the dead Christ in the tomb. All the sensible sweetness that is foregone is the precious ointment spilt out of the broken alabaster box for Christ's burial: what is left in the box is emptiness, the spikenard is there to comfort the wounded Body of Love.

That spikenard, that lovely waste is, as we have seen, one with the frankincense and myrrh poured out for the Divine Infant. The Rest of Christ in the tomb of our hearts is the sleeping of the seed in winter. The Midnight of Bethlehem is the Morning of Resurrection.

Holy Communion—the Holy Eucharist—is thanksgiving. Ultimately our trust, our faith, our peace, is all summed up in thanksgiving, thanksgiving to our Heavenly Father for His Son, His Gift to us.

Present at our thanksgiving are the angels. We enter into Christ's rest again in the presence of the angels. We are in the eternal moments in the Wilderness and in Gethsemane, when in His unimaginable humility, Christ leaned upon the comforting of His holy angels. May our own guardian angels, who are with us in temptation and with us in the Gethsemane of the world's agony today, be with us in our thanksgiving, fending the flame of Christ's life in us with their spread wings, folding them upon our peace, to comfort Him in our souls. May they roll back the stone at the door of the tomb of our hearts, that, every day, Christ in whom we die may rise from the dead in us and go back, in our lives, to the world.

The Crucifixion was public; the shame, the humiliation, the mockery, were seen by the crowd. Just as it is now. The Resurrection and the Risen Life was secret; then as now, to be discovered gradually and individually in each life, according to the individual necessity of love. The Glory of the Host is hidden, seen only by God. The glory of the Host-life is hidden, too, a secret apostolate, a secret Kingdom of Heaven on Earth.

There is no outward sign of the miracle that is taking place. Office-workers are bending over their desks, mothers working in their kitchens, patients lying quietly in hospital wards, nurses carrying out the exacting routine of their work of mercy, craftsmen are at their benches, factory workers riveted to their machines, prisoners are in their cells, children in their schools. In the country, farmers rise with the sun and go out to work on the land until sunset; the farm wives are feeding, milking, churning, cooking for their men and their children. Everywhere an unceasing rhythm of toil, monotonous in its repetition, goes on.

To those inside the pattern of love that it is weaving, it seems monotonous in its repetition, it seems to achieve very little.

In the almshouses and the workhouses old people, who are out of the world's work altogether at last, sit quietly with folded hands. It seems to them that their lives add up to very little too.

Nowhere is there any visible sign of glory. But, because in every town and village and hamlet of the world there are those who have surrendered their lives to the Host-life, who have made their offering daily, from the small grains of the common life, a miracle of Love is happening all the time everywhere. The Holy Spirit is descending upon the world. There is Incarnation everywhere—everywhere the Infant Christ is born; every day the Infant Christ makes the world new.

Upon the world that seems so cruel, mercy falls like summer rain; upon the world that seems so blind, light comes down in living beams. The heart of man that seems so hard is sifted, irrigated, warmed; the water of life floods it. The fire and light of the Spirit burn in it. The seed of Christ-life, which seemed to have dried up, lives and quickens, and from the secret depths of man's being the Divine Life flowers.